Advance Praise for Ho Learning Isn't Easy

"*Homeschooling When Learning Isn't Easy* is a refreshing look at special needs homeschooling. Heather's honest viewpoint cuts through your concerns and refocuses your mind to see everything that can be possible, after all. Inspirational and relatable stories will convince you that special needs homeschooling is indeed successful. Bring those special ones home; you can do this!"

Gena Suarez
Publisher, **The Old Schoolhouse® Magazine**

"**There is nothing better than being permitted to ride along on someone else's journey, and making the joyous discovery that it is very much like your own.** Heather Laurie allows us to take an intimate look inside her family's homeschooling journey, complete with significant medical and educational challenges. If you have a child with a medical issue, or serious learning struggle, **you may feel that no one understands. But Heather and her children get it.** They've been there. Even now they homeschool with medical challenges so significant that hospice is involved. So it is no small thing that Heather has allowed us to peek over her shoulder as she begins the homeschooling journey, faces many tough choices along the way and emerges with a vibrant and successful school and family experience... all the way through to transcripts and graduation. There is much to be gained by going along for the ride. Thanks, Heather, for permitting us the privilege of tagging along!"

Carol Barnier
Author of *How to Get Your Child Off the Refrigerator and Onto Learning* and *The Big WHAT NOW Book of Learning Styles*
CarolBarnier.com

Homeschooling When Learning Isn't Easy

"*Homeschooling When Learning Isn't Easy* is an encouraging look at how to successfully homeschool your special needs child all the way through high school. Heather shares the good and bad of what this journey may entail. New homeschoolers will feel empowered to walk this journey with their child. **This book should be read by all families with special needs before they make educational decisions.**"

Penny Rodgers
Blogger at Our Crazy Adventures in Autismland
ourcrazyadventuresinautismland.com

"**Parents of special needs children will be encouraged and informed by Heather's wonderful book.** Whether you are considering home-schooling, a newbie, or have been at it for years, Heather's extensive experience as a homeschooling mother of special needs children will be a help to you! I've been homeschooling my six children since 1997. We have two dyslexic kids, plus one child with a chronic medical condition. Homeschooling has been a blessing to our family for many reasons, especially because we have been able to flex and customize our educational approach to meet the needs of our children. I am so glad that I can recommend this book to others that need this information!"

Erica Johns
Author of Fine Art Pages and Resource Collections
at **EnrichmentStudies.com**

Homeschooling When Learning Isn't Easy

Homeschooling When Learning Isn't Easy

helping your family **excel** with special needs

Heather Laurie

HONEY RIDGE BOOKS

Homeschooling When Learning Isn't Easy: Helping Your Family Excel With Special Needs

The author has used first names only, except in special circumstances where she has direct permission from the family. These are real families throughout the world that have shared their stories to encourage others.

This publication is intended to provide authoritative information in regard to the subject matter covered. The author is not engaged in rendering medical or other professional services. If you require medical advice or other expert assistance, you should seek the services of a competent professional.

The websites recommended in this book are intended as resources for the reader. These websites are not intended in any way to be or to imply an endorsement on behalf of the author for the life of this book.

Cover Design: Melanie Young
Text Layout & Design: John Calvin Young

Publisher's Cataloging-in-Publication Data

Laurie, Heather.
    Homeschooling when learning isn't easy: helping your family excel with special needs./ Heather Laurie
        p. cm.
        ISBN-10: 0-9863606-0-0 (trade paperback)
        ISBN-13: 978-0-9863606-0-2 (trade paperback)
        1. Home School – Education 2. Learning Disabled Children – Education 3. Parenting I. Title.
        371.9

Table of Contents

To my lovely family for putting up with mommy's late night writing binges and cranky editing grumbles. May this book show you my passion to help others so that you too may reach for your dreams.

A special thanks to Thomas. I was blessed to see you grow from a struggling child into an upright Christian man. Your passing saddens me, yet I rest in the knowledge that I will see you again in Heaven.

Chapter 1: We Ditched Our IEP!

While sitting around the dining room table one wintry morning my three oldest children Bella, Gabe, and Grace were hard at work. Our homeschooling came to an abrupt halt as my two youngest daughters Rose and Maggie, burst into the room. The girls had sparkly dress-up clothes on with ribbons tied in their hair. They were dancing and singing to a Veggie Tales song. Everyone at the table jumped up and joined in the fun. Singing and dancing a parade of happy noise through the kitchen. It was a high energy break from our morning's studies.

My oldest daughter scooped up little Maggie, two years old at the time, and held her on her lap. They were clapping and cheering on the parade. The kitchen was full of laughter and fun.

Suddenly Bella's scared voice cut through the din, "Mom! Look at Maggie," her sharp, panicked tone silenced the room. I could easily see from across the room there was something very wrong with my youngest daughter.

She was lying stiffly across Bella's lap. Her eyes were rolled back in her head and she was shaking all over. She was having another seizure. Proof that my dearest little one would not be spared the harsh medical symptoms of our genetic illness, mitochondrial disease.

Choosing to Homeschool Through It All

My family is not your typical family. There is no disguising that we are dealing with a variety of special needs. We walk a different path than most because of our unique needs. The medical strain we are under naturally cut us off from many in our community, our circle of friends and family.

Homeschooling When Learning Isn't Easy

We feared for a long time we were on a path so far from normal that we were utterly alone. Then I started my blog www.specialneedshomeschooling.com and simply asked if there were more homeschoolers out there dealing with out of the norm issues. Are there others homeschooling with special needs? I found there are many, many families dealing with a multitude of issues as well. We were not alone!

When you are born with a disability the cards are stacked against you. The world is becoming a more disability friendly place but the simple fact is there are problems we have to face each day. Learning, mobility, visual problems that can't be worked around they have to be tackled or accommodated for. All too often in the struggle to find the right path for our child, we lose track of the person because we're focusing on their disabilities and needs.

Envision with me an enriched, loving, safe environment where your child can learn all the things about life safely and at their speed, from academics to life skills and the ability to pull it all together in order to become a Godly productive adult.

Homeschooling Can Give Your Child That Beautiful Gift!

Early in my parenting I found myself staring around the dining room table at the group of therapists, a case worker, and a small pile of letters from doctors all summarizing my daughter's weaknesses my heart sank.

Each person took turns telling me where her delays were and how much therapy would be needed to try to correct it. While some tried to encourage and uplift, the majority of that meeting was aimed at her delays and faults. They missed the who we were talking about, my precious little girl that loves cats, tons of books.

The way my state's Early Intervention (birth to 3 home therapy team) works several members of the group sitting around my table would go on to be our IEP team for pre-K. I realized rather quickly that the main job of several team members was to get my daughter ready to not cause a problem in a pre-K classroom setting rather than set goals for her life.

That seemed backwards to me. Shouldn't we be finding her strengths and weaknesses and addressing them to help her with the autism? Shouldn't the team be focused like a laser on helping her day to day struggles so that her frustration levels would lower and hopefully her communication abilities raise?

How is it helping to find ways a 3 year old can sit in a chair for long periods of time? My husband and I felt that spending therapy time preparing my daughter for a classroom to sit and be quiet was a waste of her time, our time, and theirs. We changed from merely following the team meekly to leading the therapy team towards life goals we felt our daughter needed to achieve.

This therapy team was a tool to be used to get my daughter needed therapy in specific areas. Then we were going to branch off on our own.

We were determined to homeschool our daughter taking into consideration her unique combination of autism, mitochondrial disease and giftedness. Including the additional stress of having siblings with similar learning and medical issues. Crazy, I know but we knew that this is what our child needed and we were going to find a way to make it happen!

Special needs would not be a way to label and limit my daughter. Autism, giftedness, medical fragile were not going to be labels slapped on a mason jar that our daughter would be stuck into. She was not going to be stared at for descriptions of a small part of her overall person. Nor was she going to be trapped by those labels. My daughter was going to be taught to dream big and live life to the best of her abilities.

It was a change in thinking from treating each pop up symptom to seeing the beautiful whole child. She was having a rough time. Language regression, stroke, autism, and mitochondrial disease. Yes, things looked dark, but there was great hope. Her father and I knew there was so much more.

Homeschooling When Learning Isn't Easy

Just as she was my responsibility to raise, care for, and nurture so too was her future in my hands. I needed to keep the big picture in mind. The dream that outshines the here and now and is filled with big promise. I needed to help open her to the possibilities that might come with a brighter tomorrow.

When her time in Early Intervention therapy was over with a light heart I ditched the IEP, therapy team and the paperwork that went with it all and never went back. Even when my sweet little girl had two more sisters that needed therapy and intervention for the same disease we chose to not return to the paperwork mill for state therapy assistance. I was wise to the paperwork and labeling system in place and chose a different route. A unique path that was crafted with each the big picture and the whole family in mind.

We went off the beaten path and our entire family has flourished because of it!

Walking a Unique Path

We are special because by today's standards a family of seven is huge. Possibly because we have homeschooled all our children and happily continue to do so all the way through graduation. Or is it the autism, learning disabilities, or mitochondrial disease that 6 members of our family have to deal with. Maybe it's my obsession with white boards? I am not sure and frankly I have given myself the freedom to not care.

We are a uniquely blessed family that has no need to stop and look at what culture declares we should be doing. Or what limits our disease should be placing upon us. I realize that it is my responsibly and honor to raise my children to the very best of their ability whatever that may be. Each day has its ups and downs but we keep going. We persevere.

Have I always been this guilt free and upfront? No. Frankly don't let me fool you. There are times I see another child or cousin of the same age doing things that my child can't and get choked up. I stop and question where we are and if we should be doing more or less. I think that this is a healthy thought process. We need to be evaluating and reevaluating where we are and where we are going. However let's not get lost in comparing apples to oranges. Learning to love your child's uniqueness is part of finding peace and creating a healthy homeschooling atmosphere.

The path to where I am today has had its ups and downs. Over ten years ago when we started our homeschooling journey I was in a very lonely and self-questioning place. I feared for a long time that my family's homeschooling path was so far from normal we were utterly alone.

Were there other special needs homeschoolers? Did other moms wonder what was going on with their child's late reading? Questioning should my child go to public school so they could get more therapy? Also when do I officially start "schooling"? What curriculums are out there for special needs homeschoolers?

Then I started my blog www.specialneedshomeschooling.com and simply asked if there were more homeschoolers out there dealing with out of the mainstream issues. Are there others homeschooling with special needs? I found there are many, many families dealing with a multitude of special needs issues.

We were not alone! You are not alone on this special needs homeschooling journey!

Dana, a homeschooling mom, told me "I wish I had known that it would be this easy, this much fun, this amazing of an experience. I wish I had known that it would help to build a relationship with my children that we would never have had if we had chosen not to homeschool. I also wish I had realized sooner that I have 365 days to cover materials and that means I don't have to teach every subject every day."

How Did You Get Here?

Parents are seeking options other than a public school system that is not living up to its promises and failing the most tender of our children. Homeschooling is becoming that safe option for many families.

Homeschooling When Learning Isn't Easy

It is quickly growing in the United States. Homeschooling is education based out of the home normally taught and directed by the parents instead of a public or private school.

Does your child have a chronic illness causing too many missed days of school for doctor appointments? Children with immunity problems are defenseless against the onslaught of germs a normal classroom has. The very real possibility that your child could become gravely ill unless removed from that setting is a strong reason to homeschool. Medically fragile children often have multiple specialists that require regular appointments.

The number of days out of school can become a huge burden. Even when those days are accounted for by doctor's notes, some states require parents to appear in truancy court to verify those excused days. Parents are realizing that if they are going to be out of work for all the sick days and all the administrative days they may as well quit and start homeschooling. Go home and begin learning in a much less stressed and supportive atmosphere.

Is your gifted child learning asynchronously and you worry about whether or not they are being taught to match their abilities? Recent budget cuts made my state stop all of the gifted funding leaving very little money to fund extra teachers and outings.

Where does that leave children that are champing at the bit to learn more, more, more, more! That means mom and dad are left having to fill in that need for more learning every day in the few hours after school between homework and sleep. If you are already bridging the gap educationally why not take full reign of your child's education and homeschool? When learning at home your child can excel at the ability and speed the Lord has blessed them with. Instead of arguing over a 10 year old taking a high school level science class, just buy it and go!

Perhaps the IEP you spent hours helping to hammer out is not followed no matter how hard you push?

We Ditched Our IEP!

What a frustrating position. You did everything you were told to do. You have been emailing back and forth with the teachers and special needs coordinator for a couple of months now. You might even consider some of the team your friend. The reality of enacting the IEP never happened or only partially occurred. We all must find that line in the sand where it is no longer acceptable to put off your child's needs for the next meeting, or the next round of emails. There are legal ways to appeal but frankly your child needs assistance now. Embrace your parental rights and step forward to get your child started immediately on the best path to overcoming and remediating their special needs.

Is your child telling you they want to be homeschooled? Listen with an open mind and heart. If your child or teen has come to the place they are asking for homeschooling there is a reason.

They may need a time of rest from the endless hamster wheel of social pressure. They may need time to catch up to speed educationally after a particularly hard year. Kids tend to self-regulate and find the best method for their learning and happiness if we allow. If we give them the space and enriched environment to show us.

Many of us walk down the same path of trying to balance what is best for our child and where best can they get their education. Reasons like special needs, religion, strengthening family ties, and many other reasons can lead us to the place where homeschooling is an unexpected but viable even desired choice.

This Is Not Your Mother's Homeschooling!

When you hear homeschooling, what is the image that comes to mind? Is it a solitary family cut off from community activities? Children that shy away from strangers like outsiders are ravenous wolves? Uber geeky kids that have loads of book learning but no sports prowess and trip walking down a flat road? Then meet the new face of homeschooling!

Homeschooling is a success! Homeschoolers are actively sought out by many of the top colleges throughout the nation. Homeschooled children often top national bees and major tests like the PSAT, SAT, or ACT. Our children grow to be productive, highly educated, often very involved in their community as adults. The opportunities for homeschoolers are ever expanding as the ranks of homeschoolers swell and education about the validity of homeschooling is spreading.

There have been years so packed full of activities and groups meetings that I had to learn the word no. Mommy group meetings for the little ones. Co-op classes for the older kids. Going to meet with their friends and build forts out in the woods. If you have the gumption and desire, there are many opportunities in your community both around you and online that your child can participate in to further their learning options.

Homeschoolers of today meet regularly for support groups, play groups, and group classes called co-ops. Local businesses such as karate studios that would normally be vacant during school hours have caught on and are now having homeschool classes. Opportunities are growing for homeschoolers of all abilities across the United States.

A child with special needs will find that the homeschooling community is welcoming and curious, in a good way. In general homeschoolers are very understanding. A child's age does not equate to their intellectual ability or their behavioral ability. The homeschooling community does not generally have a judgmental atmosphere about what your child should be doing as per age or grade expectation. Homeschooling is all about parental choice and pursuing learning at your child's natural rate and ability.

What Exactly Does "Special Needs" Mean?

The more I researched the term special needs and what it means in education circles and to the world in general the less clarity I found on this issue. Everyone had their own version of what a "special needs child" meant. Some I asked believed that everyone is special, the term "special needs" is just a label and therefore not a good thing. Others I talked to believed you have to test x number of times at a pre-determined percentage to verify if you are special needs or not. For each person or resource I found there was a different definition. I want to be clear up front with what I consider special needs in homeschooling.

Having a special need is when your child is not progressing in the normal age/grade expectation that you typically see in your local public school. This can mean children that are excelling well past those expectations, gifted, or those that are struggling to learn the basics. There are even tricky kids that are like mountain peaks and valleys in their ability levels with highs and lows all in the same wonderful child. I also consider those that have medical issues that disrupt their life and learning ability to fall into the special needs realm.

Then there are special needs families that have a significant special need in the immediate family. As homeschoolers I add a parent's chronic illness or disability because that will directly impact a child's learning environment and how they are taught. Parents, don't feel guilty about your illness or adding a loved one to the family with a significant need.

See this as another learning journey. Teaching empathy, caring, health, and emotional fortitude under difficult times. All these lessons will make for a stronger more capable adult someday.

Special needs should not be used as a label to contain what your child can achieve. Saying your child has a special need is more a way of describing a behavior or learning issue that you see and want to address. I have seen families deal with acute special needs such as cancer in the family or a car accident while continuing to homeschool. Other families deal with more long term issue like autism and chronic medical problems. Given the right attitude and support these family thrive with homeschooling. Special needs issues happen to most families whether in an acute circumstance or long term. The homeschooling is a tool we can use to make the transitions and learning about life through these hardships a better experience.

Why Families Choose to Homeschool

The reasons to homeschool are as varied as the families. The most often cited reasons are the poor quality of public schooling, the social dysfunction seen in schools, the desire to have the family unit strengthened, traveling, religion, and of course special needs.

Homeschooling is completely legal in the United States. Each state has laws that govern how you need to legally homeschool. State officials may ask for paperwork showing your intention to homeschool your child, attendance records, grades, or very little paperwork depending upon that state's laws. It very important to know that it depends on the state you live in for your specific situation.

Special needs children are generally included in the overall homeschooling law. There are some exceptions to that generality. There are a few states that require extra paperwork or testing to show proof of progress. We will talk about this later and how you can successfully homeschool even within the toughest state legal requirements.

The ultimate gift of homeschooling is that it is customizable for each child. If your child needs to slow down and repeat the fundamentals of math you can, while accelerating in reading. You can change how your child is taught to more fully involve them in the learning. You can delve deeply into a subject rather than just skimming the top and memorizing a set of numbers and facts for a test.

Homeschoolers strive to understand the hows and whys of the world. Teaching a love of learning along the way is a high priority for many, including my family.

Horizon Expanding Kids for Veteran Homeschoolers

Are you the family that has successfully been homeschooling for several years and now child number three learns nothing like the rest? Then you have been blessed with a horizon expanding child. Your homeschooling groove that you have been using is probably never going to be the same. That doesn't mean you need should allow yourself and family to be frustrated and quit. Together we are going to find out how to best meet your child's needs while keeping your whole homeschooling family progressing and running peacefully.

We Ditched Our IEP!

What you are seeing in your child's learning might be a different learning style, a maturity issue, or a possible learning disability. If you find out the Lord has blessed you with a child that has special needs you don't need to stop homeschooling. The special need can be incorporated into a new vision of homeschooling for your family. The big picture might have to be adjusted but it is still there and it is still glorious!

Homeschooling Later on in the School Years

If you didn't join the homeschooling ranks on the first day of Pre-K or Kindergarten that's okay. You might be surprised to know that because of the acceptance of homeschooling's ability to help your child when they begin struggling or face concerns with the school they are attending parents are pulling their children and teens out of school from Pre-K day 2 all the way up through Senior Year in high school.

It can be an incredibly hard decision to make.

I say, "Good for you!" I applaud you for deciding to change when you felt the need to. It is a very hard to change the path of educational inertia. Once in the public school system and the platitudes that next year will be better are thick in late May. IEP meetings that are full of appeasements to parents for what wasn't accomplished. Or worse to blame parents and keep them quiet and submissive.

On the whole, I think that teachers feel that they will be able to help your child but so quickly your child is just one in a classroom of many others that all have separate needs with limited time and energy to meet them all. Your child may just slide further and further down the list and not get the education or the one on one time needed to excel.

Are you concerned that you might not be accepted by the rest of the homeschoolers? Will homeschooling parents be snobbish and not allow your family into their co-ops and groups? Since you are the "new" kid at the co-op or support group meetings.

You will be fine. Homeschooling is all about parental choice.

Homeschooling When Learning Isn't Easy

The homeschooling community has a wide variety of people involved all walks of life, religious beliefs, and ages. Some homeschool just for kindergarten, some homeschool K-12 and beyond, some pull their child when they feel there is a need and homeschool them and then send them back to a brick and mortar when they feel their child is ready. This is your choice.

Don't Panic!

Homeschooling sounds interesting but there is a lot to think about. Special needs families can add an extra twist to the normal questions homeschoolers face. Can we handle one paycheck and still get our gluten free groceries and co-pays on top of the average expenditures? Can I handle the emotional drain of being everything to my teen that is a "line of sight" only teen due to safety concerns? Emotionally dealing with a child that has significant issues can be incredibly draining and we are going to look at how to alleviate those concerns. Questions of retaining therapy, specialized tutors, and IEPs also need to be addressed. Even questions about the future, "If I start homeschooling can my child ever return to a public school?"

Homeschooling a special needs child can be incredibly helpful! You can be certain to have subject specific learning where you pick learning material just for your child's unique strengths and weaknesses. You can have a more intense therapy schedule if necessary. If your child needs multiple doctor appointments instead of missing class and losing ground you take the learning material with you. Your child will be less stressed and anxious at home. They will be exposed to less viruses. You can provide a one to one environment that is necessary for many kids to learn.

Together we will walk through how to start your homeschooling journey. I will show you how to handle your child's school withdrawal, finding books, and learning material. Those that have an urgent need to withdrawal your child I will help you with chapter 5, Homeschooling 911: When You Have to Start Homeschooling Now!

We Ditched Our IEP!

Homeschooling with special needs has been a wonderful family enriching experience. We are pulled together by our struggles rather than apart. We have found a level of peace and success at home that amazes the kid's doctors and those close to us. I believe whole heartedly that homeschooling provides a wonderful unique education that is able to meet all your child's needs.

Chapter 2: You Are Not Alone!

"Are you looking for the OxyLearn of the educational world?" Insert a picture of a child struggling over homework, clearly having a horrible time. The announcer breaks in with, "Just try this guaranteed to fix all lagging subjects or your money back. Use every day and in just 1 short month your child's learning disability will be gone!"

Cut to scene of child hugging their mom, "gee mom, thanks for getting OxyLearn! I know everything now!"

Sorry to get your hopes up but OxyLearn doesn't exist. Not in the homeschooling world, the local private school, the public school or the pricey computer program. There are those out there who are willing to sell you OxyLearn, or rather their version, for a hefty price.

There are also friends, relatives, even the man at the grocery store all believe some magical fix can be found in the school down the street. You should immediately put your child into public school they say. I have heard so many variations on how the schools here, or near the big city, or in the charter school can cure your child's learning disability.

If your local school system could cure learning disabilities wouldn't the world be knocking down the doors to that school? The richest of the rich would be bringing their children with learning disabilities to that school to be cured. They would line up a mile long just to get that cure for their child. I don't see the stampede do you?

It may seem an extreme example but it's a true to life example. We were told repeatedly that we needed to put our child with dyslexia back in school and she would be reading within a month. It was very upsetting at the time. All we desired was support while helping our daughter overcome her learning disability. Instead it felt like we were getting let down and told our decisions were the ones that created this learning disability.

Later, after having a child attend public school with a similar learning disability, the same person that argued with us about our homeschooling saw that there was no cure. That the school system tried but had limitations, we as homeschoolers were not bound by. Being able to compare that to my daughter the difference was night and day. The school system pushed the other child to the point of tears and a serious dislike of all things to do with reading and learning. My daughter while she still struggles with reading and always will, now enjoys reading for pleasure.

I believe that when faced with something out of the ordinary, like homeschooling or special needs, people can say the silliest, strangest, and sadly sometimes the cruelest things with good intentions. In our case the comments were meant to help and over time we mended that fence.

Homeschooling not too long ago, I sat in my chair looking across the dining room table at all the bowed heads as they worked on their assignments. At that moment I had my oldest teen watching a video on "Euclid, the father of Geometry" down to my youngest daughter who was working hard on writing and sounding out a page of simple words. I never quite imagined our journey in homeschooling to be as rocky, quirky, and fulfilling for everyone in the family, myself included.

What a blessing it is to see the sparkle in your child's eye as they read their first word. Especially when the journey to get there took years longer than expected. The rough times when you held your child and cried with them because the work they were doing just a few weeks earlier was no longer "in their brain" due to a seizure that snatched moments away. As a mother I am in awe watching my children change and grow.

As I look at those lovely bowed heads hard at work I see the beauty and unique qualities of each child and I marvel at the gifts they have. Each have different strengths and weaknesses that no one else in the world has. Put all these children together and you can change the complexion of the family, community, or even the world!

As you and I raise our children, I pray that we are raising them to fulfill the unique abilities the Lord as blessed them with. I also pray, that at the end of our homeschooling journey we produce Godly adults who are productive to the best of their abilities.

A Glimpse Into Your Homeschooling Future

What will homeschooling your special learner(s) look like? Let's start with windows into other familie's homeschooling and see what homeschooling is like for them. Let's look at how unique each family is. From the style of homeschooling they choose to the schedules that works the best for them.

I have been blessed with 5 children. Four of my lovely children are on the autism spectrum. All five have sensory integration disorder problems. Learning issues go hand in hand with mitochondrial disease, the unstable genetic disease we share. Our home can be intense at times.

Intense yes, chaotic generally no. I think we have a vibrant life! I have found a place of peace and balance in our home that makes our lives enjoyable.

One of the first things I was discovered when we started homeschooling is that learning is not confined to 8am-3pm. Learning and life intermingle so thoroughly that you and your child are soon life schooling. Things like life skills become day to day living and learning. This can be one of the most useful things about homeschooling a child with special needs. They don't have to generalize a skill learned in a sterile classroom to then try to fit it into home life. You start in home life and use the skill as it will be used the rest of their lives. The ability to fully integrate life and learning ends up creating life schooling.

Life schooling also includes the delightful ability to live life to the fullest today. No hesitation. No waiting for vacation time. Field trips can happen when you pass a sign that says, "Fort Pitt open today, Free!

Noon to 5PM". Suddenly you have a great history field trip. Free fits the budget, and with signs out the historical team at the fort is ready for interested groups of people. Time to go off lesson plan and learn out of the box. Life schooling at its best!

Is Homeschooling Possible?

Absolutely! Homeschooling a child with special needs is possible. It is a responsible choice. It is successful!

Homeschooling my children with special needs has been a delight; it is legal and I don't need to have specialized certifications. I don't even have to rely on the school system to get therapy for my children. We follow the law and provide all paperwork required by my state on time and in order. After meeting our legal obligations we choose to go our own way and care for the needs of our children privately.

*I will speak more on legal issues later. I do need to remind you I am a mom not a lawyer so if you have any questions regarding your specific state or family please ask a legal group like HSLDA[1] the sooner the better.

There are other practical aspects of homeschooling you might be wondering about such as money, time, and emotional support when dealing with an intense situation. At first I had rose colored glasses on about homeschooling and felt that everyone would just understand and come to support us eventually. I thought that therapy would be a passing problem and our health in general would improve as I changed out diet. However reality is our (later diagnosed) genetic disease will never go away and only gets worse. Therapy will be needed on and off throughout our entire lives. The emotional support I felt would come flooding in one day? It never came.

We have support but no big shout out to the world, "they were right to homeschool. I was wrong for making fun of them." Go ahead and laugh. Somewhere in my head I wanted to hear that but only for selfish reasons. I am happy with the way things stand now. Our loved ones either fully support us or are neutral about homeschooling. Our friends if they made it through the gauntlet of us have a family full of catastrophic illnesses, high medical need, autism, and homeschooling are pure gold! The others can be ignored, although it is easier said than done at times. In the end you have your family and if your family is comfortable in its own homeschooling skin than you can make it through any ups and downs.

Lay It Out Practically for Me

Homeschooling takes time. Time yes, but not nearly as much as you are imagining!

My first vision of homeschooling was having my daughter working from 9 o'clock through late afternoon, just like the local all-day kindergarten. We would take breaks for lunch and a recess out in the yard. What I quickly realized was my kindergartener could not attend schooling for hours on end, nor did she need too.

I soon found that it was close to impossible just to keep her in her seat for five minutes. We were homeschooling in part because of her possible ADHD so I was open to changing. If she could get the work done, I didn't care if she was standing on her chair or sitting. Short intense bursts replaced long winded examples and even longer worksheets.

I realized that when it was one on one teaching long hours of schooling were not necessary. If you consider a school day. There is a lot of paper work for the teacher to fill out, attendance, grading. Teachers also need to pay attention to about 20-30 children. Then there is shuffling children to the gym, to the lunch room, out to recess, and don't forget potty breaks. All this takes time, lots of time the more kids you have to shuffle. The average child in school will spend a great deal of their time doing things that have absolutely nothing pertaining to learning.

At home we can focus on nothing but learning for shorter bursts of time. While working any questions that came up and answered, any mistakes corrected immediately. Instead of practicing to get the idea, you practice to the point of skill mastery.

I tell my kids to this day, "We don't work to boredom. We work to mastery!"

Does that mean your child will always be perfect? No. It does mean that if your child is writing their letters wrong you see it and address it immediately. This is particularly important for black and white thinkers, like a child with autism. Then our wonderful children and teens that need repetition will get it and they will get it correctly each time even if they are 15 or 21. We are here to teach our children and that comes with no age limit.

Life has moved on and more children have come along to fill up some of those quiet moments. The schedule changes as each child gets older and needs more time to really delve into a subject. While I do not homeschool all day long. I must devote a larger amount of the day to learning as the kids grow.

Homeschooling a Kinetic Lego Learner

A fellow homeschooling mom I look up to stunned me when she admitted she began thinking about quitting homeschooling soon after *starting*. Her older children started in public school but for her son things were not working. He is a highly kinetic and auditory, high energy, out of the box thinker so the classroom setting was the exact opposite of his learning style.

Michelle, a fellow homeschooling mom, told me that when she tried to fit their homeschooling into other people's mold she wanted to quit. She thought that to be a successful homeschooler meant she needed to have a traditional homeschooling schedule of wake early, use textbooks, and workbooks. This was just not how her family functioned. They all became frustrated and discouraged.

Michelle shared her best advice was, "Don't try to recreate the classroom at home. Let go of that. I don't want you to give up!"

You Are Not Alone!

When her son found the Lego League team and started to shine. He excelled at robotics and soon was so uplifted at his success he became self-taught in high interest subjects. Homeschooling wasn't just wonderful for Michelle's son it helped the whole family. His younger sister happily began learning material that was graded years above her head but by learning it kinetically with fun as the focus.

Michelle was not only homeschooling her children she was also a WAHM (work at home mom). She had a home business so nonscheduled events popped up often. It was difficult to plan long term. Their family's homeschooling schedule adjusted to meet their needs. Nighttime homeschooling was not out of the ordinary. Hyper focusing on a specific topic and being delight driven in their learning pursuits helped. The final bit of the puzzle occurred when Michelle realized that she had a night owl for a son.

Yes, it is perfectly okay to start homeschooling after dinner. I know of several families that do! We do. My teenagers seem to come out of their shell later in the night.

Michelle and her family began to excel and flourish when she found that, "Structure created frustration for us."

Her son has now graduated homeschooling and college. While in college he did need some accommodations for his ADHD but the college was happy to work with him and everything worked out fine. Homeschooling a child that learns and thinks outside the box is absolutely possible!

Homeschooling Is a Responsible Choice

When you are considering homeschooling a child with special needs or you find out your child has a previously undiscovered learning issue there is often resistance to homeschooling. Some have a knee jerk reaction that you need a special certification to teach. There are even professionals that will insistent homeschooling a child with special needs is illegal. Homeschooling your child no matter their strengths or weaknesses is perfectly legal in the United States and most places around the world.

You can and will be able to create goals and an educational plan for your child. You don't have to make an IEP like document to be successful! I am going to share my secret to how I have homeschooled five children all with special needs for well over a decade.

Let's look at another family and how they have found homeschooling to be a responsible wonderful choice of educating their children. Here is a family with two sons and two daughters. Both sons have autism. While they do deal with an IEP for one child and therapy for both that is not the focus of their life.

NORA'S FAMILY

Nora shared, *"We are radical unschoolers. There are very few typical days around here but we incorporate similar elements into each week. Each child has some of their own activities- one son has therapies, another has playdates, one daughter has scouts and 4H, the other has karate and drawing class and so forth.*

As a family we incorporate an afternoon at the gym for swimming and an afternoon to volunteer at the dog shelter. We have a family wipe-board where we document ideas about things we would like to do and add those to our week as well (recent ideas were the aquarium and snow tubing and horseback riding and visiting grandma). We still have a good amount of time at home where the kids can get involved in their many interests or spontaneously something will attract their interest. I will support and facilitate their efforts."

Nora tailors the learning enriched environment of their home to her children's special needs and abilities. She, like all homeschoolers, takes the time to recognize and meet her children's needs. Whether that is an online high school class or finding a speech therapist. Homeschoolers take on the responsibility of educating our children, including meeting their special needs.

Nora does point out that, "there is no 'they' –no one is going to pave the path to homeschooling for you, it's going to be rocky. There is no guarantee that there will be a community to hold your hand. You have to be steadfast, have faith, and trust your child".

Community is one of the main reasons I started writing about special needs homeschooling. I wanted to help create a strong healthy special needs homeschooling community. My hope and purpose in creating my blog www.specialneedshomeschooling.com is to help you keep homeschooling.

Homeschooling Your Child With Special Needs Is Successful!

When I first started homeschooling I had developed this beautiful dream image of the family 14 years down the road. Our daughter heading off to college years early with top grades and ability in all subjects. She was a Rhodes Scholar; star of the downtown theater, working on various volunteer projects on the weekends. Working at various volunteer projects on the weekends. She would also become an Olympic athlete. I dream big. All her siblings would be lined up behind her ready with similar resumes to their names as well.

The first day of homeschooling I had lined up neatly a box of crayons, a set of simple workbooks, and a rounded pair of scissors. I had been reading books and even attended a support group already. We were ready to go.

How did I get to those huge dreams? I read lots of parenting and homeschooling books then lumped all the best parts of the books together. I created wildly unrealistic standards to hold us against. Then when we began experiencing more than the normal amount of problems with reading I got very upset.

Chris and I never stopped to consider there being a problem between the here and now of a very young kindergartener and graduation. In our plans our daughter would fly through her education. We were more worried about what we would do with a very young teen ready for college than we were in teaching phonics and how to tell time. Our focus was on years in the future.

The first week was not nearly as successful as I thought it would be. The next week was worse. I thought it was my daughter's attention span ability causing problems. I would just crack down and be more authoritative. No help. Alright then I will change the book we were learning out of, three curriculum changes later still no good. Then it must be me. I am the problem. I was a homeschooling failure. The first few months of homeschooling were a quick correction back to reality. I had to stop thinking about years from now and focus on the here and now.

Phonics and coloring in the lines.

I was frustrated and lost. I stopped reading books about homeschooling because I was so upset by their fabulous outcomes and all I could see were our failures. My failures. I saw my worth as a homeschooling mom in the reflection of my child's grade. I didn't hold my child to that silly standard but guilt held me to it.

We bumbled through a couple more months of trying to teach my daughter to read. The change happened when my husband and my mother both told me about their trouble with reading. They were both dyslexic, so is my lovely daughter. Now I realized that our daughter was not only struggling with ADHD she also had dyslexia. I accepted we were a special needs homeschooling family and were going to have to look outside the curriculum box for learning success.

My Secret to Successfully Homeschooling 5 Different Special Needs Learners

I first came up with subject specific learning out of the need to address our faltering first year of homeschooling. Using my daughter's strongest learning modes to teach to her weakest subjects. Subject specific learning also focuses on keeping in mind exactly what I am teaching and how. If I am teaching history then my daughter didn't need to read the book. Her weakness in reading would soon overwhelm the lesson and no history would be learned but frustration towards learning and history would probably grow. Be specific to the topic you are teaching rather than trying to make your child generalize and use several skills all at once.

I knew that my daughter tended towards kinetic and audio learning. I looked for K level reading systems or books that used kinetic or audio as a basis. At the time over a decade ago, I could not find what I was looking for so I took what we had and morphed it into a kinetic and audio reading curriculum. Today there are many more options that will make your life easier.

I am so glad I took the leap of faith to begin teaching my daughter outside the comforts of the normal book. She slowly but surely learned the alphabet that year and began working on phonics. My approach was to use the knowledge I had of my daughter and how she learned then applied that to helping her overcome dyslexia.

Time passed, lots of time, as in years. Yes, it took years for my daughter to be able to read and comprehend the written word. It was not easy and she will always fight some aspects of reading and dealing with dyslexia. However she is doing a great job!

She has become a young adult that is successfully able to deal with her dyslexia. Not only has she had to deal with dyslexia but my dear daughter had a stroke like episode. Mitochondrial disease caused her to miss the first week of homeschooling her junior year, lying in a hospital with electrodes hooked up to her head getting MRI scans. It was a nightmare that took months to recover from.

My daughter is my hero. She worked on relearning what she forgot. She has grown up in a family with others that have significant health issues. Helping everyone and loving us as we needed it over the years. Then when her stroke occurred she didn't give up. She fought her way back up and kept going.

One of our main objectives in allowing her to progress at her pace in reading was to preserve her love of learning and reading. We always had some form of language arts geared towards helping dyslexics but we never pushed her to a pace the local school or another child who happened to be the same age would adhere to. When she was a senior in high school I asked on the first day of school for each of my five children to bring me whatever book they were reading. My daughter brought me *Pride and Prejudice* with a small smile.

You earned that smile my love!

The Big Picture

When you found out you were having a little one or the letter in the mail came saying the adoption placement was set, you had a big dream. It grew in your imagination over time and it was wondrous. Now that we are parenting our children and the bumps and curveballs of life are here that big dream should continue to be just as glorious.

Adjustments may have to be made along the way. Our vision of a child that would jaunt off into life at the age of 18 may be unrealistic. Or a child that loves reading as much as we do isn't going to happen because dyslexia makes the act of reading too hard.

What is your goal for your child? Are we aiming for college prepared automatons that blend in so well with their public schooled peers no one will know we homeschooled? Could we be just trying to hang on until our child grows out of some of the behaviors and we are in survival mode? Where did that big dream go in the midst of a messy reality?

I think it is right there in front of you waiting to be rediscovered. Homeschooling allows us to go at our child's natural pace and development. Creating a lifestyle of living and learning a great life!

It has taken me time and unfortunately some parental mistakes to realize that I quickly bought into the idea of wanting our family to be normal. We aren't. Who needs normal anyway?

You Are Not Alone!

Normal isn't something we strive for? Each of us are beautiful and unique just the way the Lord intended. I have found a special peace with that. The big dream is alive and well for each of my children and it is planned not by me but by God.

The end result of years of homeschooling will be a young adult that is Godly and productive to the best of their ability. Whatever that maybe. Whether they are gifted and leave for campus at the age of 12 or they will live at home with us for the rest of their life. I choose to follow the path the Lord has set before my precious child and someday when they are able to turn the big dream over to them to let them create beauty in this world.

---

[1] HSLDA, http://www.hslda.org

Chapter 3: Creating a Successful Home-school Groove

"**T**aking attendance." That phrase makes me think about children sitting in hard backed chair/desk contraptions. *Little House on the Prairie* style and me with a high neck starched shirt, my hair pulled tightly back into a bun, ready to start my one room schoolhouse. School marm ready to start the day with the sun.

I clear my throat to call my class to order. Open my lesson plan book and call out, "Laurie, Gabriel" my son mumbles, "Present".

"Laurie, Grace"

"Here" yells a child from the hinterlands of the living room.

"Come on. Get in here we need to start on time today. Laurie, Isabella, present" but I note with a raised eyebrow she is checking her email.

"Laurie, Rose."

"Here" comes a muffled response from the floor near the window, where she and her little sister Maggie are playing cards in a sunbeam on the rug.

At this point even my imagination can't keep a straight face and we devolve into our normal silliness, "Wait, are you two still in pajamas?" From there on out it just gets more abysmal as our huge Ragdoll cat, all twenty-seven pounds of him, jumps up in the middle of the table with pencils and papers flying, to get his morning pets. Kids start squealing and giggling.

Starting on time is not one of our strengths.

Homeschooling When Learning Isn't Easy

Let's face it, the Laurie clan is not a prim and proper group. We are a laughter filled, fly by the seat of our pants, fun loving bunch (pets included.) A pioneer style one room schoolhouse could never contain us. The only thing pioneer style about us is our love for travel.

I had better leave the straight-laced attendance taking to the professionals. I am so much happier with how we live and learn. I have no desire to stop homeschooling after more than a decade. We would clearly be able to show that we "attend" homeschooling regularly but it would most likely not be what a non-homeschooler or public schooled person would expect.

We homeschool year round rather than the 180 day public school standard. Homeschooling allows us the freedom to count Saturdays at the creative arts museum as the learning experience it is. Therapy and specialized tutoring as education. Attendance in big chunks of time put together to learn or small chunks of time that are slow and steady. Helping our children work towards mastery of learning and skills.

I have realized however that I do need to track out learning. We have considered moving to other states that are closer to our medical care. They would require more paperwork to legally homeschool. There is also the need to keep track of a semester's worth of work for college admission purposes. The simplest way to do that is through attendance and grading.

Frankly there is a need in homeschooling to keep a paperwork trail. Special needs homeschoolers tend to be held to a higher standard. Also our higher than normal interactions with the medical world could leave us open to professionals that feel that they can "for our own good" interject state officials in our home life. Keeping paperwork protects us whether that is attendance, therapy notes, or educational evaluations this paperwork shows what you have done or plan to do. If you were ever to get a call by the school system or other government agencies to prove you are teaching your child then you can show that paperwork trail as proof of learning.

Creating a Successful Homeschool Groove

First let's get the legal stuff out of the way! It truly is one of the foundational blocks of your homeschooling. You need to follow the laws of your state to protect your family's ability to continue homeschooling. Before we get deeper into the idea of paperwork and meeting state regulations I need to remind you I am an M.O.M. I am not a lawyer and I strongly encourage you at any point you feel that you might need legal guidance or are having unpleasant communications with your local school system call a lawyer or lawyer group that knows homeschooling law in your state.

Don't Be Put Off by Paperwork!

If you are called to homeschool, then do it! The laws and paperwork appear to be one of the most daunting parts of homeschooling but let me assure you the paperwork is not as difficult as it looks. You don't have to be an extraordinarily organized person, or a person that has the whole year planned out from day one. You do however need to have a plan and the wisdom to start early.

There are many different laws pertaining to keeping records of your homeschooling and your child's progress. I can't say it enough, know your state's homeschooling regulations and follow them! If you need to take attendance each day or for a certain number of hours than do it! Should there ever be any question then you can show the authorities that you have fully complied with the law. Let me assure you there are many homeschoolers successfully navigating the law in your state and you can too.

My simple rule of thumb when it comes to paperwork is this: if I were face to face with the superintendent of schools could I truthfully justify the time I have written down. Don't forget that learning happens at Karate practice, a three day tour of the Smithsonian Museums, or a week long science camp, just like it happens in the backyard digging up worms to draw them and learn about their biology. We don't teach like a school. We don't have to. If you can look at the superintendent and say yes my child is learning to the best of their ability then you are fine.

A word of warning each state is responsible for their own laws and interpretation of those laws. However, you must remember Facebook and other social media crosses state lines and things can get testy! A homeschooling article spreads at the speed of the share button. Soon everyone you have ever known from elementary school to the local neighborhood garage sale gives their 2 cents about your homeschooling. They don't know the law like you but that hasn't stopped online drama before. Knowing your state law and adhering to it will be the best stress reliever you can have. You are doing the right thing for your family. Time to walk turn off the computer and walk away.

Your Specific State Law Is What Is Important

I started this book telling you all how "We Ditched Our IEP" you can imagine how I feel about aggressive laws requiring heavy paperwork and medical professional documentation. Cumbersome and overburdening to a family that is already dealing with more than your average family. For those that wonder, there is no link between how many laws a state has to watch over homeschooling families and how homeschooled children excel. Researchers have looked into this numerous times and states with looser regulations, such as Alaska, have homeschooling students that excel at pace or better than the state with more onerous laws.[1] It's the parents that end up dragging the weight of more paperwork around.

Get a copy of your state's homeschooling laws. After more than a decade of homeschooling in the same state and school system I still have a copy of my state law in my easy to reach paperwork file. I feel that I am responsible for having a current law at my fingertips so I know the law and can refer to it. I am also careful to realize that any official I work with may not be as aware of homeschooling laws as I am. Having the copy of the law helps keep us both on track.

Other ways to be aware of the paperwork your state requires is to join your state support group. State groups keep up to date on any considered changes to that law or adjustments in the interpretation of the law. It is always best to start from a place of knowledge. If you know your law then you can be positive that your family adheres to it precisely.

When learning about your state laws you may hear about church schools or umbrella schools. These are actual private schools that are allowing you to homeschool under their supervision. For many families dealing with special needs this can be a wonderful option. Many states require standardized testing at every grade or certain grades throughout your child's educational career. An umbrella school could help you legally navigate through those years without taking tests that are not reflective of your child's abilities or for children that are too significantly disabled to take tests.

NOSEY NELLIES AND THEIR COUSINS: MEDICAL NOSEY NELLIES

The basic Nosey Nellie is the person at the grocery store that questions why your child is not at school. Then they question your child "who was the 14th president?" Or they make nasty comments loudly meant for you to hear. Sadly that means your child also hears. While you may have to talk with your child on the way home from the store. This instance will be a passing issue and you probably won't run into that person again.

Your family and friends could be Nosey Nellies too. The comments start small. Biting little snippets about how if your child was in school they wouldn't be struggling. Worse they start the "I remember that you stunk at spelling too." Implying you are the reason your child is struggling with spelling because of your teaching. Instead it may be that you and your child have the same learning disability but it was never diagnosed in you. Family and friends are generally closer to your heart and therefore their comments have more weight. Their slights hurt worse. The boundaries that are easy to put up with someone you don't know are much harder to erect and stay in place with your brother or mother in law.

Then comes a special breed of Nosey Nellie, the Medical Nosey Nellie. These are the people we come into contact with while dealing with everything from therapy to intense hospital stays. These people like our family and friends can be wonderful and helpful to our children. But we are talking about the Medical Nosey Nellies the slim few that feel their positon as doctor, therapist, or even medical administrator places them in a position to judge.

Run-ins with Medical Nosey Nellies are usually instances of uncomfortable questioning of your education and parenting decision that crosses the line. Like I took a teen into see our pediatrician. The appointment was going well until the decision on vaccinations for the early teen years was brought up. I felt that my teen should have some say in this decision and her answer was a resounding no. With mitochondrial disease our specialist had given us very specific instruction on all aspects of care including vaccinations so we brought up that protocol letter and asked for another vaccine for that age which my teen thought was a good idea and I agreed. The doctor was noticeably angry.

The doctor did as we asked but at the end of the appointment she told my daughter to call her anytime day or night when she finally felt she could talk freely. The final report for that day noted that our choice of homeschooling should be reevaluated. You can guess we never went back to that doctor, but nothing more than that nasty moment happened.

Normally, that is where it stops but there are a few cases when the Nosey Nellie just has to push it. They call child services. I have heard of families that have had to deal with child services because a medical professional felt they had too many children and had been to the doctors too many times that season. Families being turned in for something as simple as they wanted to take a break from aggressive therapy over the summer. They had every intention of restarting therapy in the fall but the therapist didn't ask them. She decided she had to call to clarify the situation by using the state child services.

I have had to deal with a child services investigation because a person on my child's therapy team didn't understand mitochondrial disease. Instead of taking the recommendations of the other team members, some of which had been with us for years, she called child services. This team member could have easily had a conversation with the mitochondrial specialist via Skype or over the phone. A team group meeting, but communication was not her strong suit. I find that to be a common problem with Nosey Nellies that push too far. They are uncomfortable with being forthright. They don't want to have any form of confrontation or open questioning so they call someone else to do it for them. If you find a person on your child's therapy or medical team that is like that I suggest you find a replacement.

In general Nosey Nellies will be more a stress problem than an intrusive investigation problem. Speaking as a person who has dealt with an investigation and had it cleared up in days you need legal protection. Find an umbrella legal protection group and buy a year's worth of basically legal insurance. Such as HSLDA, the Home School Legal Defense Association, who assisted my family in our time of need.

I had my lawyer on the phone while the case worker was at the door. We talked via the cell phone and my families' rights were clarified. The worker was professional and did not push beyond his jurisdiction. That calm professional demeanor by all helped the case be cleared up quickly.

Planning Your Homeschooling Journey

Write your reason to homeschool and your yearly goal down! I have our reason and yearly family goal written down on in the inner front page of my lesson book. Our vision statement is there to turn to on a rough day, a great day, and those unfocused days when you wonder if you are doing the right thing. Having these two important things helps in two major ways. One it reminds you that you have a thoughtful well-reasoned choice to homeschool. That may be as simple as "this is the only way I can keep my child safe from bullies" or have nothing to do with a special need like "the Lord has called us to train up our children." Some years we simply wrote scripture that we felt was our guiding purpose in homeschooling. When the Nosey Nellies of life come along and try to pick you apart, having a written reason to be homeschooling will stop them in their tracks.

Secondly, write out your goal. As a teenager I shot for the Jr Olympics team in women's handgun. You don't just shoot blankly down range with no target. If you did you would not know how close to the bullseye you were. There are times you have to adjust, but if you don't have a target to aim for you will not know which direction or how much adjustment is necessary. Don't make your life harder and more frustrating by not having these two important steps in your homeschooling foundation worked out.

There is no wrong way to plan your homeschooling journey! The key is to be comfortable with your plans. Should you choose to plan out your entire year in August or make a general structure and adjust as you go, or are you the live each day and find the learning along the way just be confident enough to choose what you feel works best for your family and go with it for at least 3 months. When I asked on the Special Needs Homeschooling Facebook page it became clear the answer was based on our like or dislike of structure.

If you are the meticulous type, desiring to be highly organized you may feel much safer and more comfortable with a lesson plan clearly marked for the entire school year. If you embrace an unschooling philosophy which flows from day to day learning from your natural life experiences, you will most likely not have plans. I homeschool about the middle.

I am what would be considered a relaxed homeschooler. I have a structure and goals for the year. I have a defined structure to our year and it gets more detailed the closer we get, such as the coming 8 week cycle or more detailed for the coming week. I found that planning in a very detailed fashion, months in advance tended to strangle our natural sensory breaks and delight driven learning ventures. Soon the lesson plans were driving the homeschooling rather than us experiencing learning. We have changed our style of homeschooling many times through the years and it has not hurt the overall progress of learning. Remember we are here not only to homeschool but to keep the love for learning burning in our children's hearts!

Structure of Your Homeschooling Life

Time to begin thinking about the function and structure of your schedule, how to run your home, and even how to carve hours a day out to homeschool. Finding a new way to look at learning and living that is more integrated and peaceful will be part of this process. Homeschooling will help you create a lifestyle of enriched learning and a loving family that will lead you to a less stressed more peaceful home.

Ami was kind enough to share a slice of her family's homeschooling journey with us. Her son is exceptionally gifted and deals with dyslexia, auditory processing disorder, dysgraphia and Celiac disease. They started their educational journey in the public school system but after that failed her son they left the school system. They chose homeschooling.

Ami told me, "I had no clue how to teach in a way other than what I grew up with (textbooks, rote learning etc) I didn't realize how much literature and projects could aid the learning process. I didn't understand how to work with an "out of the box" kid, one who surpassed me in two subjects by the time he was 10 but struggled with skills (handwriting, phonics, etc) that seemed simple to me. Most of all, I wish I had known the beauty of "breathe, mom. It's all right."

Homeschooling When Learning Isn't Easy

Her son found it difficult to learn how to read using traditional methods. The beginning reader materials like phonics workbooks, readers, and textbooks were so frustrating he absolutely hated them. Ami decided to instead read classics, kids adventure series, and much more on a daily basis.

Ami got a wonderful surprise when, "About a year and a half later, when he was nine, I got sick and lost my voice about a third of the way through the Hobbit. He was so bummed that he would have to wait to hear the rest of the story that he asked if he could just read it on his own. He completely shocked me.

My response was "I don't know can you?" He answered "Well, I wouldn't ask if I didn't think I could" so he picked up a Tolkien novel and read it inside of a week."

Here is a family that chose no formal therapy (at the time of this interview) but saw wonderful results through persistent hard work and out of the box thinking. That does not mean his learning disabilities were not real or went away. Mom says that at times they still rear their head especially when he is sick or tired. Overall her son now has a firm understanding of his learning disabilities and the knowledge of how to deal with them allowing his exceptional intellect to shine.

Routines, Schedules to Make Your Home Run Smoothly

Our home runs on routines. We have ones that are set in stone like "Stinky Chore Tuesday" which becomes "Taco Tuesday". Sounds weird, I know, but makes perfect sense to my kids. Wednesday is our trash day so on Tuesday all the stinky chores like the kitty litter have to be done and trash needs to be taken out to the curb. If the kids all pitch in and get their stinky chores done then dinner will be "Taco Tuesday". We have routine like that for many things in our life. Routines are things that the kids don't even have to ask about because they know it is part of how our family works. Everyone gets showers on Saturday and sets out their church clothes: it's an expected part of life. These routines help my kids learn independence and how to be an integral helpful part of a team. It also keeps down on the repeated questions a mom of five has to deal with.

I have homeschooling routines as well. Such as every Sunday I spend an hour or 2 with the lesson book and preparation for the coming week. I make sure the last week was completed and everything we needed to get done was checked off. If we need to repeat anything I write it into the upcoming week. This is my time to print off worksheets, coloring pages, poems, etc. It's when I make sure that all the books are where they are supposed to be and get out our extra material like paint, games, yarn. I find that if we start Monday with everything pulled together and ready to go the whole week starts on the right foot and things flow better all week long.

Schedules are more time based. We start homeschooling at 9 am. Then it runs daily on a "work day" schedule from Monday through Friday. We have a "rest day" schedule for days that are not homeschooling days. Just in case we also have "sick day" schedule for those rough days. Right after my stroke, when I was extremely sick, my husband would teach new concepts and do experiments on Saturday. Allowing me to be more of a guide to the children during the week rather than face the need for intensive teaching.

I have to admit I have never had a schedule made out for the whole year by September 1st. Until recently, lesson plan books and I had a hairy relationship. I don't start the year blind but I generally just have the Eifel tower like structured outline to our school year rather than the Taj Mah Hall all detailed and filled in. We use a schedule of 6 -8 week cycles that are generally designed around the science or history units. Each cycle is basically set but each week is fleshed out on Sunday in detail making allowances for each child's special learning needs because there are times the children excel faster than expected.

Scheduling is a good thing if used wisely. If I have the weekly schedule ready to go the everyday low grade stress and grumbles go away. The kids are happier too. Your children soon know what and when to get ready for learning time. As for a monthly schedule a general outline of where you start and where you end in your books is helpful. This gives you a heads up to increase of relax your pace and whether or not you need to get more material.

Homeschooling is highly adaptable. Families work out a wide variety of schedules and timing of their school year. Don't feel you have to stick to the September to June model of the public school system. Remember you are homeschooling and you are the person in charge of setting the schedule, pace, and material your child learns. We year round homeschool because it is what works best for my children. This helps my children keep going slow and steady. I don't have to deal with summer brain drain. For many children with special needs this slow and steady all year round method works wonderfully.

Don't slam shut the book and run away! There is a trick to year round homeschooling and yes you do get lots of breaks. We homeschool all morning, leaving the afternoon for big projects, field trips, co-op, or just being a kid exploring the backyard. We take breaks about every 6 to 8 weeks for one week, except during the holidays where we take a longer break. Finding the routine, schedule, or system that works best for your family is important. I can present you with options and ideas to help you homeschool as effectively and successfully as possible. Enjoy and take with you only the best to create a peaceful, learning enriched, and loving home.

Outside Pressures on Your School Year

Back to my funny pioneer visual about taking attendance yes, some states do require you to take attendance. This can appear daunting when you are starting homeschooling but it is very possible to accomplish. When you layer in that you are dealing with special needs the paperwork for medical or state disability requirements things can start to appear insurmountable. Fear not my brave friends we can take care of this paperwork mountain with ease and a bit of preplanning.

I start tracking our homeschooling paperwork on July 1st every year. Why would I start taking attendance in the summer? The biggest reason is to give us breathing room. The more days marked off before the cold and flu season all the better for us. I never know if one of the kids or I will be hospitalized for several days and this gives us breathing room to work while staying legal.

There are other pressures that shape our planning and schedule. Outside opportunities like a Co-op, instrument practices, or sports can require you to adjust your schedule. If you pick a curriculum that requires teacher interaction like a cyber school, or an online academics program then you will need to be more structured. There are also various products or programs that come with very specific instructions on use to be fully effective and compliant with their rules.

Take the long view and remember the big dream when planning. When my kids were younger I needed to stress therapy more so we had structured therapy sessions. Then we moved to a much less structured time where I was more focused on social interaction, setting schedules, and habits that would help me create a more peaceful home. Now that I have to consider high school credits and graduation I am turning to a more academically structured schedule again. We evaluate our children's needs each year and set goals based on what they are working towards.

Use planning, structure, and your schedule as tools to help you homeschool not to hinder you. Keep in mind the level of structure that you are comfortable and the time you can put into preparation and planning. Allow flexibility in your schedule so that if your child's needs are more time intensive than first suspected you still have wiggle room. The goal is not to tie ourselves down with more work but to uplift us by having a structure to turn to if we slow down or get off track. Plan with the big picture in mind. We are homeschooling in order to produce godly productive adults to the best of their ability!

The Home in Homeschooling

We haven't even talked about the majority of your day. What? You think you will be spending all day everyday stooped over a book homeschooling? Nope.

Homeschooling When Learning Isn't Easy

The majority of your day will not be stuck in textbooks even if you choose the most traditional methods of learning. You will be teaching one to one with your child, even if you have several children. That takes away so much of the extra fluff work and needless mistakes a child can ingrain before it is seen and corrected. You are going to be right there to adjust, correct, and your child will learn mastery of a subject or skill and can be done for the day. In my experience the homeschooling book portion of our life is done by 2pm (even with high schoolers), elementary grades can easily be done by noon. There are online schooling and umbrella schooling programs that require a predetermined amount of time per day for your child per subject. Frankly I don't like those programs at all. Our children are learning differently and that should be reflected through our daily schedule and their time on task.

I do not confine our learning to those hours though. I fully realize that my responsibility is to teach my child about life and skills that don't naturally come to my children with autism. They need therapy and life schooling. My children need to learn not only math and fine motor skills but they need to learn how to eat gluten free. Like Ami's son, who we talked about earlier, we have Celiac disease too. If I were to ignore that very important health need my children would suffer. I like that at home we can be very careful with our foods so my children do not suffer from behavioral, attention, and even long term damage like stomach cancer due to dietary mistakes.

Many families are dealing with more immediate concerns that home-schooling allows them to address, like peanut and fish allergies. Some need to watch sugars, or nebulizers and breathing treatments that must be promptly given. Homeschooling allows you to not only be very responsive to these needs, timely in the application of medication like anti-seizures but you get to teach your child how to eventually take over their own care and medication as they are able.

Your home is a safety net that many children need to be healthy, less germs for those with impaired immune systems more control of those with serious food allergies. For those with sensory issues you can design a sensory diet obstacle course they can use when they need to get the wiggles out they can without getting in trouble.

Being with our children daily allows us to have a good idea when things have gone off course. The first step when you suspect a learning issue is the pediatrician's office. Then the eye doctor, dentist (you heard me right, a cavity can deeply affect your child's attention span), and any specialist or therapist those doctors recommend.

While seeking medical help you can adjust your home to better meet your child's needs and directly meet your child's strengthens and weaknesses.

Now we are going to tailor a curriculum to fit your child and your family's needs. Using subject specific learning to meet each need and progress in a timely less stressful, less frustrating manner.

Homeschooling is a great fit whether you are dealing with a physical disability or a mental health issue. Your child is a blessing with strengths and weaknesses like all of us. Some weaknesses can be harder to deal with and behavior disorders are tough. I will not soft pedal it and say follow XYZ and poof your child will get better. I do know that seeking the problem out and dealing with it head on is better than hoping your child will grow out of it. Homeschooling means no waiting for the okay from an IEP team to adjust to your child's needs. You just do it!

---

[1] Dr. Brian Ray, *Strengths of Their Own: Home Schoolers Across America*, National Home Education Research Institute, Salem, OR, 1997.

Chapter 4: The Curriculum of Champions!

When my son was younger he couldn't speak clearly. We were put off repeatedly by his doctors telling us that "boys communicated later." "He was letting his sister do his talking." "Oh, he's just having a rough day." He wasn't. Frustration was mounting and my son was getting older and his lack of clear speech was starting to impact him socially. We fought back and finally got him into speech therapy.

What we didn't know was that early delayed speech had a wide range of problems outside of the obvious understandability and frustration issues. My son was not able to articulate phonics. His reading was now delayed. When we worked through the basics of that I realized that he also had problems understanding and hearing phonics. My son has Auditory Processing Disorder.

Basically that means that his ears can physically hear sounds but the brain isn't sure what to do with them. One of the results can be slurred speech, because the child can't "hear" their own distinct sounds. It definitely slowed down learning phonics and reading skills. It also impacted his ability to understand what was being read to him and reading comprehension.

We slowly but surely started working through the layers of issues. Speech therapy to work on the articulation and motor skills of his mouth. Then we added auditory processing programs to help him begin to rewire his brain. The entire time I never gave up reading to him.

The problem was Gabe was not able to stay awake when we read to him. Nor could he explain what was being read to him. I found that he didn't develop the skills to make a mental movie of what was going on in the book. He didn't have an image in his head of what the hero of the book looked like. He couldn't imagine an action scene. This was not a creative intellectual problem it stemmed from his processing disorder. He struggled so much to understand the words he didn't have the time or energy left to make that mental movie we all naturally form when reading a book.

I found a great way to teach him this skill. We watched the BBC cartoon *Redwall* and began reading *Redwall*. It was a high interest story for him. By watching the cartoon and getting an idea of what the book looked like while reading the book we very slowly and steadily began building reading comprehension skills. I read it only when we were in a very quiet calm room. I would read in small bits then stop and ask him to repeat what was happening. This took months to get through a single book! When we were done we had gone from him falling asleep after a couple of paragraphs with no understanding to being able to get through a couple of pages when my son would ask us to stop so he could think about what we just read.

More years passed and more reading and hard work. Now he was able to incorporate reading out loud at the table with his four siblings for homeschooling and understand most of it. Homeschooling has given us the time and ability to work through these difficult and multi-layered problems.

How Does Your Child Learn?

I use a triangle visual in my workshops to show how a child learns. The modes of learning are visual, audio, and kinetic. The middle of the triangle is the glue that holds it together, attention, the ability to process the information, and memory to store/retrieve that input. Your child will move around the triangle during their lifetime. Most kids start very close to kinetic and hands on learning. As they grow they move towards another version of learning as their main way to input learning material.

Visual is when a child brings in information through watching it. They learn best through video, you working on a white board, picture books, or diagrams. Audio is the child that loves to hear you read everything aloud. They want to learn their alphabet via song, they hum under their breath putting review material to an inner musical score. If you were to turn on music in the background you up their ability to remember and learn. The kinetic child is one that just has to feel everything. Do everything. If there is a couch to be bounced on while reading their book, they do.

Where the Learning Bumps in the Path Happen

First there could be a problem with any of the major three ways to input information. Something as profound as blindness or a learning disability like auditory processing disorder. Then there is that pesky middle area that talks about attention, processing information and storing it to retrieve when needed later. If attention is lacking like in ADHD the information doesn't even get in. If the ability to process and retrieve the information is lacking then you will not know if you child has a meaningful understanding of the learning material you just taught. In short the triangle's glue doesn't hold it together and things strain. Learning suffers.

You can see what happens when all these things are working and working well in a gifted child. They have a large capacity to intake information from multiple ways. They can store the information very efficiently. Then as needed they can reproduce accurately that information in a useful timely manner.

Learning disabilities are not new and there are therapies to address the problems. The goal of our effort is going to be first and foremost to eliminate any learning issue. If that is not possible then we will work hard towards remediating it. Which is to deal with as much as possible and any lingering issues will be successfully handled by our child as they grow. Finally, there are some issues that try as we might are not going to be able to be eliminated or remediated to the point of internal adjustments. We will need to teach our child accommodations to work around their problem. Such as dyscalculia (a problem with understanding math and math concepts) could be so significant that a child/teen will need to use a calculator, not out of laziness, but because their brain is not wired to remember the multiplication facts no matter how you try to teach them.

Should I Consider Educational Testing?

You may be asking yourself, "okay I know there is a problem, but I just don't know where the problem is". The goal with any disability is elimination, remediation, or accommodation. I try to always work towards the best outcome, elimination. If we have to stop along the way at remediation or accommodation then we do. I have had children that needed accommodations of being read to for years because of dyslexia that suddenly shifted to reading on their own. There is always hope so work towards the best outcome and always expect the best outcome from your child!

Even so you may need to know where our child stands today in a solid quantifiable way. You think that some sort of testing to find out where the holes in learning are and how best to overcome them would help. That's fine.

TESTING

Here are my general outline for when I would recommend testing:

- Your child is 2 grades behind (this could be in only 1 subject or skill)

- Your child will need accommodations for high stakes testing in high school (ACT, PSAT, SAT)

- Your child is a mystery to you and you need guidance.

- You feel there could be a legal problem. (SSDI, divorce, protective services investigation, medical team interference)

- Your child feels depressed about learning issues or feels like they are dumb.

The Curriculum of Champions!

If you go for any kind of educational testing, I highly recommend private testing. I know this will cost more but it is for your use only, it will be for you only and not go into your child's file at the county school board. Also the school's evaluation testing and therapy is set up to help a child in a classroom setting. For us, when we attempted that route it was frustrating and I felt that in the end it would not be enough therapy to help my child live a full, well balanced life.

You should expect a large packet of paperwork to fill out about your child learning as it is today. Including basics on medical history. The testing itself should be involved and designed to push your child to their limits over several hours or even a couple of days. Yes, this isn't easy to see but it is necessary so the evaluator can see how long your child can maintain attention, what kind of sensory issues they have, or if there is a developmental component to your child's learning issue that needs to be addressed.

The final test results should be hefty. You should get information about where your child's weaknesses **and** strengths lie. You should get a clear statement on how best to address the weaker areas, therapies or reading systems that work best for your child's very specific issues. Finally this should not be based upon what that clinic, therapist, or doctor does in their clinic. If your child would excel with the Orington-Gillingham reading program than an honest evaluator should tell you even if they don't offer that program.

Now that you have a firm grip on what is going on it's time to create a curriculum that is going to address those needs. We are going to pull together learning material that not only helps your child excel with their strengths but deal with the weaker areas in a pointed manner. We are going to create the curriculum of champions!

I have been blessed to raise five children all with special needs due to their mitochondrial disease. My homeschooling world revolves around dealing with learning disabilities to major medical issues. Through the years we have been able to eliminate some issues. I have been able to remediate and help my children come up with internal ways to deal with their sensory issues so that they can be independent and self-regulated.

There are also some issues that are not going to go away but need to be adjusted and use accommodations. I needed to find a way to teach all five kids at once without losing all my hair and being positive that each child gets the attention their unique learning issues require on a daily basis. I created Subject Specific Learning.

What Is Subject Specific Learning?

It is learning that is tailored to your child's special strengths and weaknesses. This means each subject is looked at separately. You decide what learning level your child is per subject and skill. You decide what learning style your child best responds to. Then you see what's available that fits those criteria or take an existing curriculum and adjust it. The end result is all subjects and skills get equal attention and tailoring to meet your special learner's needs.

That sounds like a lot doesn't it? The hard work is up front and will be worth the effort. Together we will step through this process and create a curriculum that helps your child excel. In the end your child will be less stressed and more able to move forward and progress with this specialized curriculum that we are going to build!

Step one is to get a good feel of where you child is per subject. If you have a previous IEP or educational testing then look at the paperwork. They should clearly state where you child is in all areas of education and major life skills. If you are like me and pish posh for most testing then you can go to your state education website for their "standards" per grade level. There are many other sites and books that will give you the basics for what skills need to be acquired per grade.

One warning here: the first time I looked up my child's grade level requirements I was overwhelmed. The state educational system's website broke everything down in minute detail so there were pages and pages of standards. That was scary enough but then I started reading the standards and some were silly easy others were years beyond what I imagined a typical child could perform. The moral of the story is: use your common sense while reading through the material

The Curriculum of Champions!

and know that some standards are there for standardized testing not a true picture of what a 2nd grader should know.

Let's get back to creating a homeschooling curriculum fit for your child. Take each main subject math, history, science, reading, writing, and language arts. Give each subject a basic grade level. Highlight any learning disability you know of or specific problem for each subject, such as mark reading with dyslexia. That way when we are looking for material to match your child's needs you may have to go outside the normal homeschooling circles to find a curriculum to fit a child with dyslexia.

Now what type of learning does your child best respond to? Remember the modes of learning we talked about earlier? Visual, audio, and kinetic. We will be matching your child's weakest subject to their strongest learning mode. On the flip side in order to help your child grow and learn in a balanced manner we will be matching their strongest subject to their weakest learning mode. This should help our child move ahead in a well-rounded manner. They will be better able to deal with learning at college or at job someday.

Nora said, "I carefully considered what types of arrangements will best fit my children's level of skill and how much (and what kind of) support they will require to be successful. We also seek out therapies that will give the kids the readiness and skills necessary to be in social situations (such as counseling, OT, Therapeutic riding, speech)."

Now as we move ahead and start picking curriculum we need to be very specific and focused on our goals. What are we trying to teach our child? My son from earlier was being read *Redwall* and falling asleep just a couple paragraphs in. When I started *Redwall* it was with the intent that my son and I would take turns reading aloud. I wanted him to start reading on his own. I also wanted him to develop a higher level of reading comprehension. I had grand plans that *Redwall* was going to be our first literature lesson. When he fell asleep just paragraphs in day after day I had to reevaluate my goals.

Homeschooling When Learning Isn't Easy

I could teach my son reading with his phonics books and language arts books. I could not teach him reading comprehension unless we got the audio processing disorder under control. We focused on that one problem like a laser with our reading and audio processing program he started. That was our specific focus for six solid weeks, as per the program. With that sort of focused learning he leapt forward in understanding the spoken word and phonics. He began to stay awake for the book and it's a lot easier to comprehend a book when you aren't snoring! My son was able to deal with and mostly eliminate a problem that would have impeded his progress in almost all other forms of learning. Our subject specific learning of focusing on the processing disorder has paid off tremendously in the long run.

We didn't let the other subjects slip while we were focusing on processing. Math was done to jumping jacks (a great kinetic method of learning to count). History and science had lots of hands on projects because he could remember better using kinetic methods of learning. Homeschooling was very structured during that period but it was never dull and boring.

Where Are You Hiding the Curriculum of Champions?

The curriculum of champions is going to be the curriculum that fits your child's abilities the best using the tips from above. There is no magical curriculum dispenser. You are going to need to go to places like a homeschooling convention where you can see and feel the learning material. Talk to other mothers in your support group. Look at online and paper catalogues to find what fits your family the best.

Let's talk budget first. Many of us are dealing with a shoe string budget. Co-pays and one income makes for a slim homeschooling budget. There are free homeschooling curriculums online. The tradeoff is you are the one that is going to have to do the work for most of them. Lots of prep time, printing off, and being sure to double check the material for accuracy. I use freebies to supplement our unit studies and sometimes we hit a rough patch that requires more repetition so I use printables.

The Curriculum of Champions!

I love finding free or frugal learning material but I want you realize the lower the cost in general the more of your time it takes.

Your time is limited and worth a great deal. For me that means that I trade off free material for buying more structured textbooks and full workbooks. The structure of buying a math workbook makes sure I don't miss key foundational material. It also keeps everything together and organized without me having to pour myself into prepping every week. Since I am a special needs mom that is chronically ill and have had to hand over homeschooling to my husband when I went into the hospital many times this sort of structure is worth the money spent. My husband can pick up my lesson plan book and the math book and go on Monday morning rather than delay everyone and throw them all off schedule while I am healing.

There are also specialized programs like the audio processing program I talked about earlier. There are several programs developed to help those with autism or dyslexia. You will need to research your child's specific issue to find the program that you feel fits the best for your child and family.

Carol a veteran homeschooling mom chooses a more traditional path. She shared, "We use textbooks. I like the accountability of textbooks and it seems to work well with the way my son learns. Our textbooks have a lot of hands on suggestions that we can incorporate, so it's not just worksheets all the time."

You can find all sorts of primary source material such as a math textbook and workbook to be the spine of your math curriculum. There are also great apps to supplemental learning. Videos online and streaming can reinforce what you learned that day, though I would always watch them first just in case the content is questionable. You can even get college courses for free now online!

What If You Are Blessed With Several Special Learners?

I have five kids with differing special needs. I have not only used Subject Specific Learning to help form their individual learning I have some tricks up my sleeve to make our learning easier. I do at least two sub-jects together. Homeschooling learning material is often created with a family of multiple aged children in mind. I use that to my advantage. When I use a multi-level curriculum I don't have to be hemmed into a grade/age expectation the kids can learn at their own pace.

Our structure is based on a 6-8 week cycle based upon history or science unit studies. Overall our history is broken down into 4 year cycles American, Civic/Geography, Ancient History, World/Middle Ages. I adjust the cycle so that the presidential election happens on the year with civics. That provides tons of material like debates and voting!

Science cycles Biology, Earth/Physics, Health/Anatomy, and Chem-istry. This may need adjusting at the high school level to match the science series you are following.

Using the 4 year cycle makes sure we cover everything several times over the course of my children's homeschooling. It takes the stress out of trying to decide what comes next year. History and Science are the two easiest courses to make into group subjects so again my load is lightened in making decisions. The courses are set but even with that cycle there is a lot of leeway to go where your interests and each child's needs lie. I can do this all while the whole family is learning the same basic material, such as Egypt. I just make sure that each child has ability appropriate goals.

How to Measure Progress

When you are in charge, you are responsible for measuring prog-ress of your child's work. No matter what style of learning your homeschooling is using, we have to have some form of measurable, quantifiable progress indicator. First and foremost for our child and ourselves. It helps to know midway through the year though you feel like you have been on a hamster wheel you have actually been making great progress in writing or learning how to dress. Frankly you also have to have measurement of progress for the Powers That Be, that could mean your local school district or developmental pediatrician.

The Curriculum of Champions!

They all want to know if homeschooling is working for your special child or not. If you have taken the time to collect the learning material throughout the year to affirm your decision to homeschool not only will you be less stressed but you will be able to quickly put to ease any possible suggestion that your homeschooling is not appropriate and progressing at your child's ability (note, I didn't say the world's timetable or age/grade standard!).

The first and most effective way to show your child is progressing and homeschooling is to keep a portfolio of their work. Keeping a portfolio of your child's work is clear indication of progress and hard work throughout the year. Keep everything you do and file it. Then if necessary you can go through the work and show work from fall through spring. Not just final products but the hard earned in between lessons and mistakes. Everything from the beginning of a concept through understanding and applying the concept.

Other items that will help show progress are videos and pictures or your child working with you on an app learning to communicate. Gather things like pamphlets from places that you take your child to for field trips and write in journal form what you did. These will be wonderful mementos years to come and again they show that your child has a full and enriched life with homeschooling.

I keep medical reports and therapy reports as clear objective reports by an outside medical professional of progress either attained or attempted. These I keep in a separate file because of the possible delicate nature of the health information. If needed they are within easy reach to show that we are getting all needed assistance to help my children with their special needs.

Grading Has a Place in Homeschooling

You do need to calculate through some means whether or not your child has passed each subject. Normally through subject testing, grading paperwork and effort. Understand that in your local school the tests are usually only one-third of the total grade. Don't short change your child's efforts and work throughout the year. It all counts towards a final grade.

There is no harm in simply using a pass/fail. You can progress your child at the rate you as their teacher sees fit. During the elementary years for my children I was very open about their grading. I simply homeschooled for mastery of foundational skills. When they understood the concept we moved to the next. Spiraling ever upward always progressing. It may have looked like we were running a race with snails at times, and we were. Then other times to my sheer delight my children would surprise me and we would surge forward.

I didn't grade my children in elementary school. I only started in middle school because some of the online work was designed with testing in mind. I would correct all their work but not assign a letter grade. As my children became teens I realized that for purposes of transcripts, college, and being able to handle high stakes testing they had to move to testing and grades. We did so slowly and usually I started in their strongest subjects first so they could feel the surge of doing wonderfully and getting a high grade. Then I moved to other areas of their learning and taught them how to handle poor grades that didn't reflect their true understanding of a subject because they didn't take into account their learning disability or like any child they didn't study and got a poor grade and that too needed to be carefully addressed for some children because of anxiety. Even though they clearly could have done but better I had to deal with the issue delicately so the next time they tested they didn't shut down and give up after one failed answer.

In school, a special needs child is not necessarily passed on grades. Often in the early years they are passed on age. Your child would be passed along again and again without understanding and without a true education occurring. Homeschooling is offering your child a brighter future and a more attainable set of goals. No matter your child's ability the love to learn and act of trying is rewarding. This will help create a teen and later an adult that doesn't give up. That reaches out past the disabilities they deal with to a better self whether they are in 2nd grade or 27 years old.

The Curriculum of Champions!

Some parents are required to use standardized testing and they use them to see if their child has progressed or not. This is the least used and least reliable method for our special needs children. While many kids excel at tests, for some, testing does not show the true intellect and abilities. Be careful when relying on any one method of progress indicator. Our special needs children seem to delight in thwarting our best attempts to quantify their abilities and rate of progress.

Some Quick Tips to Keeping the Paperwork Straight

I have five children to keep straight. The best way I have found is to mark a set of file folders with the months July through June. A set for each child and I color code them per child. Then at the end of the week I put all their loose paperwork and art either in that file folder or I have an oversized legal box. I also print off the week's work of any online program we are using and add it to their file. Much of their learning material is contained in their journals or workbooks so I just need to double check that the dog hasn't walked off with the workbook before we are ready for a new week.

I love this method. It is clear visually whose files go to whom. It is also a method where I can easily look at the folders and see if one child is not completing as much work as previously. This helps me keep everyone on a steady upward path.

I have seen other ways to keep things under control. A large three ring binder with dividers, folders with pockets, and manila envelopes with 3 holes punched into them, even scrapbooking organizational items in the binder. All these worked just like a file folder system except it was much easier to take along. For me that is a double edged sword. I would hate to get to April and lose the whole binder. The good side is for long term storage a binder would be wonderful and easy to sit and look through years from now.

Another mother shared with me that she keeps a legal filing box marked with each child's name on the lid in her laundry room on a high shelf. Each child's work goes down and into their box at regular intervals. She is not fussy about keeping things in order because she asks each child to name and date all material. The box allows her to keep those larger odd shaped projects and history timelines.

There are many ways to organize our homeschooling paperwork. I highly recommend that even if it is a simple box to throw everything into it. Even if you think you would like to move to a different method later if you don't have the work sheets and printables in one place you will have a hard time locating them again. Trust me, I have been there, don't go down this road!

My friend, you are well on your way to creating a lifestyle of living and learning in a manner that best suits your child. Your family is going to flourish with the attention and specific needs being met of each member of the family.

Chapter 5: Homeschooling 911: When You Have to Start Homeschooling Now!

The news is full of reasons to start homeschooling in an emergency. Teachers and aides caught on tape berating and mistreating special needs students; bullying by fellow students; bus drivers that treat the children in their care with no compassion or unsafe driving. Schools that are failing and states that are pulling back or not funding special services for students. Learning material that is substandard. Homeschooling is the safe haven for your child to find a high quality, healthy education.

Over the years I often wondered if I was over thinking or misconstruing the relationship between special needs parents and the school system. I was at the park with a mommy group. We were there for an end of summer picnic. I was sitting in the shade watching my little ones play and chatting with the mom next to me. She was a college student about to graduate with a degree in special needs education. Obviously my ears perked up and I was very interested in her take on education.

She told me that she had been a student teacher the past spring semester and was once again working with the same high school class that fall. She told me of a student that had finally been toilet trained the previous spring only to come back that fall in diapers yet again. She was disgusted at the parenting that mother had done over the summer.

I asked, "Did you involve the mom when you were teaching the teen to toilet train?"

The student teacher huffed, "She knew what we were doing."

I pushed gently, "When the school year ended was she taught how you had this teen scheduled?"

The mom was starting to get upset with me, "Well it's her kid she should know. We took him every 2 hours to the bathroom."

I had to ask, "How could she know if you never told her?"

The teacher and student teacher had implemented a plan to toilet train this teenager. They had done it at school. They had told the parent that they were toilet training him but never taught the mom the schedule or how they were encouraging the teen. There was no continuity of care. In this lapse of continuation of care the toilet training was lost and the parent was blamed.

I found that what I was feeling as a parent attempting to get help from the local school system was accurate. My role as a parent was not paramount as the primary caregiver to a special needs child. The teachers saw themselves in that role and subtly were reinforcing that by sabotaging the parent's role.

The student teacher never said another word to me. She got up and walked away. I hope that my point was made. You have to involve the parents with raising their own children. When that line is crossed and someone else takes on the responsibility of raising your child there is a battle for their heart, mind, and soul which you might lose.

When Do Others Start Homeschooling?

A popular time to start homeschooling for many in the special needs community is at the beginning of the year. This could be because the aide that is supposed to be helping your child has not been provided by the school. Your child is showing signs of a learning disability but when you ask for him to be tested you are told no. Tough situations like these leave the year beginning not with a bang and excitement but a dud and frustration. The need to homeschool becomes apparent for your child's future success.

Another time it is common to leave the public school system is around spring break when you realize the well-crafted hard fought for IEP, Individual Education Plan, is in flames. At these times when the failure f the system is apparent, homeschooling becomes a very realistic option to help your unique learner. During spring as the year is ending and the IEP meetings are happening may be the first time you have conclusive evidence that this past year has been a failure or worse that your child has regressed in behavior or ability. What a frustrating moment. You can channel that frustration into action.

Spring break can become spring break out!

No matter when you come to the conclusion that it's time to homeschool there are times when it is less a matter of choice and more a matter of extreme urgency for the safety of your child. You have reached the end of your rope and it is time to homeschool, now! Your cry for help has been heard. Here is the best path that I have found to remove your child from the public school system in an emergency.

I am not a lawyer so please do not take this chapter as legal advice. It is however a plan of action that can protect your child and start your journey homeschooling. There are legal organizations like Home School Legal Defense Association that can help you navigate the legalities of homeschooling in your specific state.

Prayer

You need to be clear headed and focused for the task at hand. When you are pulling your child out of the school in an emergency situation the emotions can be running high. Anger, sadness, possibly fear will cloud your mind and can cause you to react poorly.

Call on the Lord for help keep yourself clear-headed and tight lipped. Do what legally needs to be done. Say only that which needs to be said to remove your child from the immediate situation. There will be time later to file formal complaints if necessary. The focus is to get your child home safely.

You will also need a hedge of protection around your family. While most student withdrawals and homeschooling startups are unremarkable and no problem arises there are times that things do not go as smoothly. Ask the Lord for protection during this time.

Ask for strength. You and your family are starting a journey that may have some rough patches. Sometimes you may feel stretched thin and wonder if you can manage. Allow God's strength to help you through those lows. Know that the majority of your time will be wonderful, a true journey of learning and loving.

Now that you have called in backup we can get started on the basics of removing your child from public school.

REMOVE YOUR CHILD FROM PHYSICAL HARM!

If your child is in a physically dangerous situation you must take immediate steps to protect your child! It may be that your child has actually been injured, bullied, or emotionally abused by other students in the school. It may be that you feel that teachers and authority figures such as aides and bus drivers are so apathetic or aggressive themselves that a physically dangerous situation could occur. As mom and dad, you need to step in and protect your child. Your child needs you! Please stand strong and be that hedge of protection your child desperately needs.

One mother of five began to be deeply concerned about her oldest daughter, who was attending the local school in their special needs department. Mom knew that her daughter was having trouble learning. School professionals tested her showing a mild intellectual disability and ADHD, but her mother didn't feel this fit her daughter and was actively working with the school to tweak the assessment of her daughter's abilities. During this process mom noticed her daughter began emotionally withdrawing from the family.

Her daughter became sullen and hated going to school. Her demeanor changed drastically and this previously fun, talkative child shut down. This situation came to a head when the mother was called to the school to find out the special education teacher had grabbed her daughter and shoved her into a corner berating her and physically attacking her daughter. Later she found out that this was not the only time her daughter had been physically assaulted by the teacher.

That was the last day her daughter spent in school. Mom immediately withdrew her daughter from public school and put her under the homeschooling regulations in her state. The state normally has a waiting period but this was waived by the school administration for this family given the circumstances. The parents insisted that their daughter would not be coming back to school for physical and emotional safety.

This family was doing all the right things, jumping through all the hoops of testing and dealing with special education teachers and paperwork. In the end it all blew up in the delicate daughter's face and this family had to immediately move to protect her. It took over a year of recovery for their daughter to heal from this episode and years more for her to be able to put it into perspective that as a child she did not in some way cause these attacks to happen.

This is one of the many reasons why I feel we must move immediately to physically protect our children. Step in and shield your children. Stop any abuse immediately.

If the situation is urgent and your child is in physical harm, you must cause a fuss. It may be uncomfortable facing a room full of administrators and teachers and telling them they are not adequately protecting your child, but it is much better than a police officer calling you to tell you that your child has been assaulted.

In order to safely and legally remove your child in a situation that is volatile or emotionally fraught. Get a lawyer. HSLDA, the Home School Legal Defense Association, can expedite your membership in this kind of situation. Call them. Document everything, including calling the police and filing a report if your child is physically assaulted or abused. *Write down every person you have talked to about this problem including names, dates, and their responses.* Print off all emails with header information attached. Do not sign *anything* without a lawyer's opinion on it including an amended IEP. Use your iPhone to record whole conversations if you legally can in your state. You need to be sure you get as much information about the situation and people involved as you can, so that later if necessary you can protect your child and yourself from misunderstandings.

A Slower, Calmer Approach

I have been told by many parents that they want to work with the school system to have an orderly removal of their child from the school system. I agree. If there is nothing abusive or harmful occurring, an orderly exit from the public school system is best.

Working with the public school system and your child's former teacher is a good goal. It might not be possible or advisable, though. Teachers and administrators may not be aware of the homeschooling law or any recent changes to it. That could lead to asking you to do much more than is required. I have seen several times when an IEP team dragged out the meetings to – give time for the mom to calm down and give up this homeschooling idea.

If you feel your family is being pushed into signing or complying with a situation that is unsafe, not truthful, or against previous agreements, get your lawyer on the phone immediately. Seeking legal help to guide you through the situation is much easier than hiring a lawyer to clean up afterwards.

The Law and Legal Assistance

You need to know your state law on home education. I highly recommend that you find the law (usually through you state homeschooling organization or a nation legal group) and get a copy for your records. You must know that law and adhere to it precisely. There is a chance that the law may change or be interpreted differently by a new school administrator so be sure to remain current with your understanding of the law.

You know the law and can respectfully but firmly keep all parties to the law and the law only. It can be very helpful to have membership in a national legal association such as HSLDA because they can provide advice and even represent you in disputes. These legal organizations would be more helpful if brought in immediately when you consider leaving the school system so they can assist you through the process if necessary. There is a chance they will turn you down for membership if you are in the middle of a dispute.

I have been homeschooling for over ten years. We have turned in all our paperwork and evaluations every year as our state's law requires. My husband and I fulfill the law and only the law. We find no helpful reason to give more paperwork and information to the schools system than is necessary. Keeping it simple and precise helps me be sure I am giving all required information and the administrator that has to look at our paperwork is easily able to see the information they need is present.

You also need to know that homeschooling a special needs child is NOT educational neglect. We are simply choosing an alternative form of learning than the public school system. If you are leaving under duress, there may even be accusations such as "I'll call Child Protective Services on you" or "homeschooling a special needs child is illegal" that can be terrifying.

Many parents are fearful of the repercussions or confrontation that may occur when you start homeschooling. The Lord said he will take care of you! He has fulfilled that promise to us.

When a new case worker came to our house and didn't understand our rare mitochondrial disease we had Child Protective Services (CPS) knocking on our door the next day. We were covered by a legal group so I called them immediately. My husband and I had followed all the homeschooling laws to the T. Our children were fed, well kept, happy, and obviously not in distress. The lawyer from our legal protection group was on the phone within minutes. It was a nerve wracking several weeks as the paperwork was completed and references were written for us but the case was closed quickly and we were able to continue homeschooling.

I pray something like that doesn't happen to you but if it does here are some tips to keep you home and family safe!

1. The case worker or anyone with them including the police cannot enter your home without a warrant or probable cause so don't let them in.

2. Be respectful at all times even if they are not. Try to record the whole incident. Get your lawyer on the phone if you can. Have a second adult there if possible to be a witness to what is happening.

3. Never let you children be interviewed alone without some form of legal guidance on their behalf, preferably a lawyer of your choosing.

Once you have the law, read the exact law from your state legislature carefully (if there is one.) Some laws are written in lawyer speak and can be difficult to clearly understand. No problem, you can find summaries of your law and how it will affect your homeschooling at a number of state and legal homeschooling groups. The good news is that most states are straight forward with their laws and have no extra requirements for special needs students. That means you follow the law for homeschoolers whatever it is. In some states, that involves a letter to the school system telling them you are homeschooling, while in others you can simply remove your child from school with no legal obligation to tell them anything. Give your school system exactly what the state law requires. If they ask for more, say with a smile and a respectful tone, "I'm sorry this is what the law requires. We won't be providing anything else." Keep it simple and clean. The law keeps it from getting personal.

Needed Paperwork

Some states require attendance records and other paperwork to be done annually. It will help you tremendously if you get that paperwork started immediately. Staying up to date is much simpler than trying to remember a year's worth of paperwork. It is also much less stressful!

I do recommend that even if you state doesn't require it, that you keep an ongoing portfolio of your child's work. A portfolio can include samples of your child's work to pictures and pamphlets of places you go on field trips. If your child is less able and cannot do written samples, you can video tape them at various times through the month showing things like therapies they undergo to how they respond to your teaching. Record keeping is a safety net and a reaffirmation in 6 months that you made the right choice!

Let's say you live in a middle of the road state that requires a form of notice that you intend to homeschool and evaluation of the year's progress.

You write up a notice of intent to homeschool, sign and date, and deliver it to whomever your law says to – the public school or the office overseeing homeschoolers, for example. You can either hand deliver it, requesting a receipt or send it certified mail with return receipt requested.

If you send your notice of intent to a state office, you'll also need to send or deliver a withdrawal letter to your child's school in most states. Again, ask for a receipt! Then clean out your child's locker at school and high tail it out of there! You'll say something like:

> "This is official notice that Sam Student is being withdrawn from Trouble Elementary School. He will be attending James Street School, a homeschool registered under (my state) a law. Please send a copy of all records to James Street School, 123 Home Str. Jonesville, NC."

Be prepared to pay for copies to be made. It's worth it.

If you decided before spring break, you can be happy that unless the law specifically says a certain number of school days' notice must be given, every day counts towards that notice, including weekends and holidays. You do not have to withdraw from the IEP or even inform the IEP team your child will be homeschooled before you leave.

Homeschooling When Learning Isn't Easy

When you have that very first step in process, call around and get any therapies covered for your child that are necessary. If you wish to withdraw from the IEP you can simply send in a letter like

> *"This is official notice that Sam Student is being withdrawn from his IEP as of **today's date**. Please send a copy of all records to James Street School, 123 Home Str. Jonesville, NC."*

It is as simple as the school withdraw and once again be ready to pay for the records. You need not give any reason or show that you have set up an IEP for your homeschool (with the very important exception of the couple of states that REQUIRE this in the homeschooling law! Know your state's law!)

Curriculum Basics

If your goal is to get your child out of the public school immediately and they offer your child's text books for the remainder of the year, take them. If you are a long term homeschooler you just gasped... right?

Calm down, there is a method to my madness.

You now have textbooks to look over and possibly work through with your child. Many states want a clear idea of what you are going to use as educational material. Their own books should satisfy them nicely. There are other perks to this. You get to see exactly what your child was using and what level the work was at. You can more easily find out what was working for him and what was not. That will help you be able to understand where your child is starting and help you create goals for where you are going. The school's textbooks usually aren't the best solution long term, though. There are many other ways you can find material to work with. You can buy a whole grade's worth of material, but that is not a great option for special needs children since they are often on different levels in different subjects. Ideally you will use subject specific learning to create your curriculum, but given that you are on the fast track, you likely haven't gotten a good feel for what works for your child and family yet to do that. There are low cost online options that now allow you to buy a full curriculum for a year or a month. That will get you started immediately and you can individualize later as you understand better what your child needs.

Healing Takes Time and Love

Now it's time to go home and learn how to be home all day long. Hopefully you'll rekindle the love for learning without the pressure of school. I would start by reading over the IEP carefully. See what the teacher notes as your child's abilities and weaknesses. See what they believed would help your child move forward. This will hopefully give you some guidelines on what your child's baseline is. Though many times a parent has called me delighted to find that at home without all the sensory problems, with proper sugar control, or with adjustments for their ADHD, their child has easily handled not only the current abilities stated in their IEP, but the goals stated for several months down the road! Relax you do not have to have books in hand on your first day. You do not have to have lesson plans. You do not have to have a schedule, posters on your wall, and a school bell to ring in order to start learning.

Now that you have legally pulled your child from the school, it's time to do school... no, not necessarily. If you pull your child from school on a Thursday you don't have to be schooling the next day. I recommend you take some time off, whether to relax and de-school or to take the time for therapy to deal with the lingering public school issues that caused your child's emergency withdrawal from school.

This break also gives you more time to figure out what learning materials you are going to use. If your child is old enough let them have a voice in the decision, but be clear that you require the work to be done.

The idea is home educating! Learning! Life schooling!

Chapter 6: The Perfect Time to Start

Iam blessed with five children, four are on the autism spectrum. Talking milestones, developmental goals, and social skills with doctors has become second nature to me. I took my daughter (third to have been diagnosed with autism) to the pediatrician for a well child appointment. The pediatrician was new to us and flabbergasted me with her blasé attitude.

We began the same old rote questions all doctors ask at well baby appointments. How many kids does your child play with? Do they have a best friend? Like other doctors we had been to, this doctor belittled my daughter's siblings as "not counting" as friends or playmates. I would beg to differ.

I was an only child. It was lonely at times and a sibling to play with would have definitely counted as social interaction with a playmate and friend. Siblings are enforced social interactions. You must learn to share, take turns, do chores, treat them nicely, and talk to them not shout at them. All these things are social skills that must be learned and clearly count as social skills and interaction.

The more questions the doctor asked the odder her attitude got as the responses were not "typical" but they were consistent with a child that has brain damage from mitochondrial disease, a Chiari and syrinx, and already diagnosed with autism by a developmental pediatrician. The pediatrician seemed to want to undiagnose my daughter or find reasons that were normal for her behavior. Even dismissing, at one point, writing a prescription to continue needed therapy.

I get it, no one wants to see a child that has a genetic disease that is life limiting. You don't have to tell me, I'm mom. I would move Mt Everest if I thought it would cure my daughter. This doctor began trying to talk me into sending my daughter to public school which she "knew" we would have excellent results. The doctor assured me that all 3 year olds were social butterflies if I would only allow my daughter to develop in a class where there were lots of other kids her autism symptoms would fade away.

My daughter had a medical condition that is known to cause autism. It also aggravated me that the doctor was not taking into account my daughter's natural personality. She might be an introvert not an extrovert. The appointment ended with me feeling guilty that I might not be offering enough for my daughter and the doctor shrugging at my unwillingness to put my child in school.

I talked with my husband and we looked at what the doctor said. Was she right? Were we missing something important in my daughter's upbringing and therapy needs? No. We were not and we continued to homeschool. Years later as my daughter has grown and more emotionally matured I now realize that she is a natural introvert. She is the type that likes one or two friends and pours all her effort into those relationships.

It has always irked me that so many therapists, doctors, and those in society push you to have multiple friends and activities to meet other kids outside the family at earlier and earlier ages. I see this trend as increasingly creating unhappy, stressed, over extended young children and families. Were all the generations before us so terribly wrong that children tended to stay close to the family for their early years? Must we all now have social butterflies at the age of 3? Is there no longer a place in this world for an introvert?

Special Needs From Birth

Sometimes you have time to come to the realization that your child has a special need or learning disability, other times you are thrown down the rabbit hole right at birth. All parents naturally begin teaching their children from birth. How to smile. Say mama. Take your first step. Special needs families that are dealing with issues from birth or the very early years have an additional responsibility of teaching what comes naturally to other children. You are special needs homeschooling from the beginning whether you planned to or not!

The Perfect Time to Start

A friend of mine and homeschooling mother of several children with special needs was blessed once more with a little one. Betty's daughter was born and needed to go directly to the NICU (Neonatal Intensive Care Unit.) She had a very delicate difficult start to life. It took time but finally her precious daughter could come home to the farm and begin life in a large loving family.

Betty's daughter needed therapy and various specialists as she grew. However, all the professionals missed a visual problem until mom realized her daughter was flipping letters, unable to recreate simple drawings, and other similar simple tasks. No one had an answer for Betty but she didn't let that stop her in researching herself. She found a developmental optometrist a couple of hours away from the farm and took her daughter. Her daughter needed significant therapy and specialized glasses.

It wasn't easy with no financial assistance or help from the school system, and hours of travel just to get to the doctor where the therapy was held. This family pulled together and made it work. Her daughter needed therapy a couple of days a week for several months. Meanwhile she had to use prism glasses and do eye exercises at home daily. Betty knew that for this season of her daughter's life intense therapy was required. The whole family shifted to meet the needs of their little sister and it was a success! With the help of weeks of very intense visual therapy she is now doing much better with less restrictive glasses.

Betty said, "Balance is something I am always dealing with. There are times I have to drop the least important, most stressful, or least helpful thing from our lives so that we can focus on what really counts, God and our family."

My friend chooses to homeschool by using real life training and doing projects and unit studies to cover most educational needs in the early years. When the kids get older and need high school level work they focus more on specific classes and a more traditional method of learning. Their home is run on a seasonal schedule rather than the more "normal" early morning to early evening schedule. During harvest the whole family is up long before the sun, working hard all morning. Then rest siesta style for the late afternoon. Then once more back to hard work of farming and tending to the animals in the evening until late.

You will learn to create a home life that allows learning, therapy, and a wonderful life. Betty and her family are not your normal 9-5 schedule oriented family and yet it works just fine for them. My family likes to work late morning till late afternoon. Early on the time burden is much less and I found our schedule needed to be aligned with the various therapies that our four children on the autism spectrum had. Life can get intense at times but you can make it work!

Autism and Homeschooling?

Homeschooling a child with autism means you get to deal with less transitions, less out of context generalization of skills, and more chances to use life skills in the time and place they will be used such as going to the store for groceries. You will also build such a strong foundation with your child they will be more apt to reach out and stretch their wings in new and uncomfortable areas of life knowing that you will always be there. Homeschooling when dealing with autism is an awesome method of learning!

Having multiple children on the spectrum in a short period of time meant I learned fast how to deal with early intervention therapy teams in my home. I learned the lingo a child with a developmental delay gets in their medical reports like OT (Occupational Therapist), PT (Physical Therapist), and many more. I really like therapy at home where your child is more likely to feel comfortable less anxious or nervous about doing things like bouncing on a trampoline. Comfortable enough to try talking and signing their needs and wants. The downside is you are letting the therapist and by extension the state into your front room.

When my daughter got the first diagnosis of autism I immediately set up therapy. For my daughter she was young enough to be in the state provided early intervention therapy program. My son, diagnosed with autism a week later, was blessed with a private therapist that was willing to come to our home to help him. I would watch closely and take notes about what the therapist did and that became part of our daily homeschooling life.

Being an active part of my child's therapy and taking notes was invaluable. It increased the speed of my child's recovery and meeting goals such as having my daughter say "I want milk." Sounds simple to some but to others you will understand my joy! She had regressed from simple sentences back to sixteen words when she was two. Asking for anything was progress and a huge leap forward in skills.

Find Help Beyond the Home

What is therapy for? Therapy is a very specialized method of teaching a skill that for whatever reason our child is struggling with. There are speech therapists that teach general speech and articulation. Then there are more specialized speech therapists that are better termed feeding specialists that work only with eating and swallowing. There are many specialties of therapies available to your child to help them when they are having delays and difficulties.

The goal of therapy should be first and foremost, **eliminate** the issue. If that is not possible or maybe just for now you need to find a way around the problem at hand, you **remediate**. Then there is learning to **accommodate**. Just because you choose to use a communication device on the iPad to accommodate a child that is non-verbal does not mean that you or the therapist has given up the hope of learning to speak. In all our years of therapy it was an evolving process that needed repeated reevaluation and setting new goals based on how my child handled the last few weeks of work.

Sometimes the outcome was outstanding! Other times we knew that the method the therapist was using was not working. It was time to try something new. Your relationship with the therapist should be a very open one where communication flows freely. In order to stay up to date with the therapist's ideas and what you see in day to day life you must feel comfortable talking to the therapist.

Homeschooling When Learning Isn't Easy

Every state has their own version of "Early Intervention" and the rules or diagnosis that makes you eligible for specific therapies. The Early Intervention system is set up in conjunction with the school system. In some cases so seamlessly that your child's medical information may flow freely from the EI team directly to the local elementary or country special needs coordinator without signed permission from you. The offices involved are just so used to sending the paperwork along it doesn't dawn on the person doing the sending that you may have said no. This can pose a special problem for homeschoolers who wish to remain free from public school entanglement.

This can also mean those working in the system are hardwired into believing that there is no other option but public school for the children they see. I got very good at interviewing possible therapists over the phone or meeting them in person and within a short time knowing if they would work for our family or not. Most were just fine and either supported or were professionally neutral when it came to homeschooling. A few people we ran into were not as professional.

One therapist came to my home for his first occupational therapy session with my daughter. Being blessed with four children on the autism spectrum meant I was a veteran of special needs by this point. I was no newbie and our file reflected that if he had read it. This therapist was an OT and was coming in to replace our previous OT. There was a clear plan of action for my daughter but he wanted to re-evaluate. My daughter needed a weighted vest to try. While bringing the therapist up to date with my daughter's needs and answering his questions I told him.

He laughed, "I don't suggest weighted vests. When she gets to school they don't have time for dealing with vests."

"We homeschool. Please go ahead and order the vest. I was told by the previous OT that there was a vest available to loan out and try," I tried to play it cool but the smile was stretched. To say he was the most dismissive person I have even met would not be an exaggeration.

The Perfect Time to Start

"I won't order one. So let's not go there." He didn't look me in the eyes or even write down that I requested a weighted vest on the daily therapy report.

The session moved on. I was not happy. He didn't care.

Before he left I remembered that I needed another OT sensory brush for her Wilbarger method exercise to help get her sensory issues under control. "Do you have an extra OT brush? We need one."

"Oh, I don't do the brushing technique. When she gets to school they won't have time to deal with that." He once again dismissed me as he was putting on his jacket. Not even pausing to listen to my request.

Now I was miffed and I loudly and clearly said, "We homeschool! I will make the time to help her."

"You think you will homeschool now but with this many kids and autism on top you will quit." He was so self-assured and calm. While he didn't literally pat me on the head he figuratively did and out the door he went.

I called his boss and he was fired by the time he got in the car.

The first and most important rule when dealing with therapists and other medical professional is that you are hiring them for their medical opinion. They are not in charge. They are there only so long as you find them helpful and necessary. If your child doesn't like their therapist I can guarantee they will make less progress than if they enjoy and get along with them. If the doctor is constantly belittling or countermanding your opinion then you need to decide whether or not they are worth all that trouble. We have kicked very prominent doctors out of our medical care team because if they won't listen to me the patient how will they listen to the medical team? In the end what is best for my child?

Moving From Early Intervention to Specialized Preschool and School Therapies

One of my daughters was diagnosed with autism, a stroke, and sensory issues early in life. We had a team of therapists in and out of the house during her early years. Some therapy was aimed at helping my daughter to communicate. The regression in language was slowly corrected. The delays that came with autism were helped. The sensory integration issues were identified and we began helping her work towards calming herself.

Towards the age of 3 there was a subtle change from therapy for my daughter to therapy to prepare her for the pre-Kindergarden class she was assumed to be entering. The team began working less towards helping her life skills and abilities and more towards her ability to go to school safely. The situation became crystal clear to me when my daughter was evaluated by the school system for ongoing therapy and she was turned down.

My daughter's mitochondrial disease had caused a stroke less than a year earlier but because she could sit in her wheelchair buckled in therapy was not needed. I was told by the therapists that were evaluating her that while the law stated any child in need of therapy would get it, the reality of the situation was there were kids that had it worse and they were underfunded. That was not an acceptable answer to my child's needs so we went for help through private therapy.

I could have fought the therapy decision but I found there were perks to private therapy. The best one is you are in charge. That is wonderful but can be intimidating. Use your therapist's expertise to help create goals and timelines you expect to see those goals accomplished. Come into therapy and watch, participate when the therapy allows. That way you can continue the therapy activities at home.

Are you thinking about using public school therapies or specific classes to fill in gaps in education or therapy? Do you have one child in public school and one at home? This is not a guilt trip. We are all adults. Do what is best for your family. That may not be the easiest path but it will always be the best path if you have truly thought it out, prayed about it, and reached a consensus with your spouse.

I want you to realize a few major differences between private therapies and most public and private school therapies. One, schools are designed for how best to integrate a special needs child into the classroom setting not how best to help them navigate a grocery store, church service, or even their own home. Two, you will need an IEP which requires meetings, upkeep, and in a time of crisis might not be followed, such as the police being called for an "out of control" five year old with sensory issues and autism melting down. Third, your state's funding or lack of it will greatly affect the quality of the therapist your child will get, the amount of time they will see your child, and the quality of the material used. Several school systems have started contracting out to the private therapy care providers you would choose anyway. Skip the middle man and go to your local private therapist and work out a therapy care plan.

On the good side you do not have to pay for public school evaluation and therapy. We are slowly moving towards a time when homeschoolers are not considered a threat to the local school system but in most places we are not there yet. Call your state organization to find out more details about your area if you are considering using the state system for therapy. There is a great deal of hope several states are moving to a much more positive healthy interaction with homeschoolers.

The Early Years Homeschooling With Autism

Black and white thinkers want black and white expectations. Write down your schedule and post them on your wall. Take pictures of the food available and put them on your fridge with magnets. Always get the same brand and respond the same until your child has mastered that conversation. Now it's time to expand slightly, with time and maturity your child will be better and better about having variations. Your life will get less restrictive.

Early life with a child with autism means you will be spending a large portion of time in various therapies. You are ultimately in charge of the schedule. It took me years to realize that while my child did need xyz therapy two times a week we didn't have to continue this therapy all year long. We could take a short couple of weeks off during the holidays or even a longer stretch after we learned there are home based therapy curriculums available to guide us. When you do use therapy services be sure there is a set goal and timetable. Hopefully this timetable will be taking your child's needs into consideration, not the insurance company's limit? When the insurance timetable is used as a guiding factor it makes me wonder if the therapy clinic's recommendations are for profit or to aid my child. Is that the amount of sessions my child needs or all the clinic could get insurance money for?

Special needs homeschooling support groups can give you the perfect opportunity to create small, highly successful social get togethers to build social skills. My support group was going to have a tea party for the preteen and teen girls in our group. There was even a tea parlor restaurant nearby that had a private room the girls were going to use. In chapter 10 I show you how to create your own special needs support group if you need to.

Let's just attack the one big argument against homeschooling a child with autism. "What about socialization?" Your average homeschooler hears this one plenty of times. Add a child that has communication and social issues naturally and I can guarantee someone in your circle will bring this up at least once if not repeatedly. The simple fact is a child with autism will have social interaction difficulties with or without homeschooling. Homeschooling gives me the flexibility to better guide my child towards successful opportunities. Like other children with giftedness or high functioning autism that have a high interest in astronomy they will do well in an astronomy group rather than a group of same aged peers. As homeschoolers we deal with people as my child will deal with them when they grow up. The post man who delivers a box unexpectedly to your home, the pharmacist at the store we frequent are all situations that can unsettle a child with special needs. It is our job to teach and guide our children to learn how do we talk and respond to the natural ebb and flow of conversation. I would argue that homeschooling allows *better social interaction* than public school.

The Smilie Method

When your child won't sit still at all. I mean not even for a couple of minutes. You have a wiggler with high energy!

I had one. No, I *have* one but he has learned methods to self-regulate. I started teaching him those methods back before he was five. My son needed to sit still long enough to work with his speech therapist. I would be sure to schedule the therapy sessions during his best time of day, early morning after a good breakfast. Then I would be sure he went through his sensory obstacle course helping to settle his sensory needs.

When the speech therapist showed up I'll admit he was often in his favorite outfit, swimming shorts. We did what worked. Our goal was to help him speak better so that his frustration level would decrease. The speech therapist brought the key to teaching my son (and later his other siblings) to sit for brief periods of time: The Smilies Method.

A simple piece of laminated paper with three Velcro spots. Onto those spots went three smilie faces with matching Velcro. As my son attended to speech exercise he would get one smilie. When he was done with three exercises he could get up and get the wiggles out.

It was very simple but did take time for him to understand. As he was able to understand and do three smilies in a row for several therapy sessions. Then the therapist changed the rules slightly. Now he needed to sit and attend for three minutes for a smilie. Soon he got the hang of that. The next step was five minutes of attention.

When my son reached the five minute mark with the smilies he told us we didn't need it any more. He would sit and finish his speech lessons within half an hour!

Over the years I have used those same smilies for different purposes. Such as when my son was in the 4th grade he kept getting up and wandering through the house after a few minutes of work. We were having trouble finishing a single subject much less the multiple subjects that were needed. I changed our day to two sections of three subjects.

He would get a smilie when one subject was done. When they were all done he knew he was done until after lunch or the next morning.

I think the smilies work so well because they are a clear way to know what is expected of you. Also a clearly defined ending to his work. That helps Gabe keep the steady schedule he craves.

Subject Specific Learning for Preschool and Under

This early in your child's life, don't hyper focus on fast paced educational programs and big pricey curriculums. Work on all the foundational skills needed that will help your child later. I highly recommend reading out loud daily. Things like colors, letters, numbers, understanding math concepts like more and less will begin to build through play. Yes, play! Lots of it. Let you child play, play, play, and play some more.

A great source of ideas will be your child's therapists. The OT (occupational therapist) can help you hone fine motor skills using things like Q-tip painting and sensory sand. A PT (physical therapist) can help with gross motor skills that help your child coordinate their body and mind like marching to music or riding a horse. Swimming is one of my all-time favorite play exercises for all ages, it helps with their muscle strength, skills, and helps calm sensory issues!

The older you child gets the more you will naturally move towards learning things through curiosity. Most children start with a very kinetic play oriented method of learning. Work with it! Use it! Get toys that help teach colors. Make file folder games to teach numbers and letters. Make some homemade gluten free play dough and encourage your sensory defense child to touch and work with it!

I also have no problem with using online programs to begin teaching your child how to use hand-eye coordination and simple preschool concepts. Just be sure to monitor and limit screen time. Yes, I have used my phone as a calming item at a specialist's appointment so I am no tech saint but I can see how easily our kids will give up the curiosity of learning the world around them and end up focusing on a little screen where cute creatures squeal and career around just for them.

Here are more quick tips to homeschooling with your child with autism. Eye to eye contact is not required but it is a goal we strive for. I start with facing my body towards my child so they know that they have my full attention. I am quick to praise even a flash of eye contact. It helps to create a secondary method of showing your child is paying attention like having them squeeze your hand or placing their flat hands next to their paper they want to work on to let you know they are ready.

This is an intense time of life, but it is only a season and will pass. Children will grow fast and we will raise children that are better self-regulated through daily patient persistent work. You are forming a foundation that will help your child their whole life. Trust. Loyalty. Respect of self, family, and others. The perfect time to start homeschooling is now.

Chapter 7: Fixing an Uneven Elementary Foundation

Children with learning problems and disabilities all need to start with a strong foundation. If they have an uneven foundation you must as a teacher-parent guide your child back to the base level of understanding and restart from there. Clear away the frustration and disappointment of you and your child's learning failure so far and start your child's learning over, ready to succeed.

Each child is extraordinary in how they think and learn. Unique and wonderful in how they see and process the world that just because your first two children worked well with a structured textbook does not mean that child number three will be the same. It can be difficult to adapt what you have been doing for years. A child that learns in a new way might be your wild child or horizon expander. I have faith in you that you can adjust your homeschooling to better match your child's needs and make learning enjoyable again!

My fourth child was my horizon expander. She was born with many of the problems we had dealt with before. Autism, low tone cerebral palsy, one sided weakness presumed from a stroke because of our mitochondrial disease but she was much weaker than the others when it came to her immune system and lungs. That meant many runs to the doctor's office, emergency room, and hospital stays. Not to mention the bevvy of nebulizer lung medication that had to be given all hours of the day. Exhausted already things just got worse for my little girl when a significant birth defect of the base of her brain called a Chiari and a syrinx was found.

A Chiari malformation is a birth defect at the base of the brain where the opening to the spinal cord is too small. The area can have trouble letting cerebral fluid through, can squeeze the brain stem, and can even cause damage to the spinal cord from pressure. Rose had so much pressure in her spine and brain that her spinal cord split and caused a syrinx. She needed neurosurgery to correct the Chiari malformation. The neurosurgeon had to enlarge the opening at the base of her skull and break the two top cervical vertebra to add more material and it took weeks for her to recover.

Then about two months after the surgery we noticed that she was walking up and down the stairs. This was a skill she had not been able to do previously despite being four. She could walk up ramps without falling. Her writing and drawing improved tremendously. She suddenly had depth perception!

She was loving and conversational with her family. However there was a slowness to her learning ability. Her therapists and I started working on this slow processing problem when she was little. Years passed with very little progress happening. The slow processing did not increase but one layer of visual disability was peeled away by this surgery.

Many times I hear of parents noting an issue with their child like sensory integration disorder. When they adjust, overcome, or make allowances for that issue they then see there was another issue blocking learning under it. Don't be afraid of finding those layers of issues. Rejoice that you are finding the issues and are now able to address them as needed.

After the surgery my daughter had an intense year of follow up appointments, therapy, and several large tests like MRIs and EEGs. At the end of the first year the Chiari decompression surgery looked superb! She was doing so well but some of her testing showed that half of her brain was not talking to the other half. It was sending signals slower and the brain would deal with this by ignoring one set of signals. That meant 50% of what she was inputting and learning was not being processed or was not able to be produced effectively. Our daughter had also been in various therapies for years and yet learning was clearly a struggle. She was now five and didn't know her colors or shapes. The doctor told us to take her home and teach her the best we could.

Months later the therapists agreed that she was not going to progress much further. They too weren't giving up but several of them felt that in the end her abilities would be limited. Chris and I decided to take a break from intense therapy.

My Horizon Expander – Multi Sensory Teaching

After a break we were ready to start a more formal homeschooling time with my daughter. My husband and I took the reports from the therapists and we took careful note of our daughter's current abilities and weaknesses. We made a short concise list of what she needed to learn the first semester of that year (this is back when I followed the public school year's schedule). We wanted her to know her colors and begin learning her letters and numbers 1-10.

That was basically the same goal that we had had for her for the 2 years previous with the therapists. I knew that I needed to think outside the box to teach her. When facing such uphill battle I decided to start with a high interest item and teach in a multi-sensory manner. Her favorite color was yellow so we started there.

I got everything yellow in the house together for a full day of YELLOW! We have a painted chalkboard on the wall so out came all the yellow chalk. While I wrapped my daughter in a yellow sheet that had been warmed in the dryer like the yellow sun. Singing and dancing to anything that incorporated yellow. Lemonade and lemons to entice her senses. Then later while I was working with her older siblings at the table she sat next to me with all the yellow crayons, markers, and paint. That was the day she learned yellow!

I used that same multi-sensory way of teaching all the colors. Some subjects and topics are much easier to teach in such an all-encompassing way. This method of teaching did take more time to pull together a lesson plan because I had no curriculum to follow. I was following my child's lead. The return on that hard work was tremendous!

My daughter is several years older now and does not need me to teach everything in such an intense multi-sensory way. I am careful to use subject specific learning with her to keep her focused and progressing forward. She has made up so much ground in the past few years that during her yearly evaluation this little one that was once told would be limited in her abilities to learn and understand was listed as grade level appropriate!

Labels Are Powerful

Labels can be used to help and heal. They can even be used to lie and place us in unsafe situations. I had an encounter with this exact issue once at a doctor's office. I got called from the waiting room, by a nurse, to go back to the examination room. This nurse then began taking down the medical information needed to put into the computer information such as what medicines I take, my general medical history, and why I was there.

I told her, "I am here because I had a seizure."

The nurse looked up at the medical file, on the computer screen. After a minute or so of reading my file she said, "Now don't tell me that, tell me what happened instead. You don't want a seizure on your record."

I was startled! Was she asking me to lie? I had a seizure, no doubt *witnessed by a neurologist*. I was there to get help stopping them. "Why?" I asked her.

She told me, "Because if you say you had a seizure then you can't drive anymore. You don't want that!"

I don't want to be driving and you shouldn't want me behind the wheel if I did have a seizure! When I was pregnant with my third child my husband and I witnessed a car coming towards us go left of center completely into our lane. It went across a middle berm, hit the hill on our side of the road, and bounced back across the whole 4 lanes. Where the car broadsided another car. The teen driving died. She had a seizure while driving. The others in the accident were badly hurt. I held a teen that was in the car with her and promised her that I would tell her little boy that mommy loved him if she died. Thank the Lord she was only injured and soon recovered. How could I ever even imagine being the driver knowingly, even with a wink and a nod, behind the wheel of a vehicle when I too could have a seizure?

As much as I didn't want the label of seizures, I needed it. When seizures were added to my medical history emergency rooms know to look for possible seizure activity. Any medical professional will know that I am most likely to be on anti-seizure medications which can interact poorly with many other medications. And of course there are safety concerns like driving was not possible until I could prove that I was no longer having seizures.

To not be labeled for a clear medical issue was ludicrous! I don't drive and will never drive again. For myself and the people around me I needed a label, the medication, doctor, and restrictions that label placed on me. Seizures don't change WHO I am. They describe a small but important part of my health.

Educational Testing As a Homeschooler

As a homeschooler you can test or not test or even better test only certain areas. As customizable as your education is with your child, so is the testing you can chose to have done. If you choose a private tester that information need never go any farther then between you and your spouse and the dining room table.

Testing in some situations can help you relax and give your child as much time to grow and mature as possible. I know it's not easy, I have been there. I hope these tips give you some guidance as to when to consider testing and when to wait.

Over the years I have chosen a mixture of various levels of testing or evaluations for my children's learning problems. The uniqueness God has blessed each child with means some needed more in-depth understanding of a problem. While others were so obvious in their issues and how to help them there was no need to test. I was careful to always listen to the doctors and my children about possible testing. Homeschooling allows us to wait well past the time the school system would have demanded testing or in a couple of situations, we were able to jump on proper testing within days of a stroke. I am so thankful for that flexibility.

TESTING

Here is my general outline for when I would recommend testing:

- Your child is 2 grades behind (this could be in only 1 subject or skill)

- Your child will need accommodations for high stakes testing in high school (ACT, PSAT, SAT)

- Your child is a mystery to you and you need guidance.

- You feel there could be a legal problem. (SSDI, divorce, protective services investigation, medical team interference)

- Your child feels depressed about learning issues or feels like they are dumb.

In the end, parents are in charge of whether or not to seek testing that may or may not label a learning or biological issue your child is dealing with. One thing we need to focus on is a label is not a manacle on your child's foot holding them back from succeeding. A label is a description of a small portion of your child's life. It can assist others, like doctors and therapists in understanding your child's needs better A label can help you focus your search on learning materials best suited to your child.

If you feel that it's time to test, you should have high confidence in the tester, the actual testing and the professionalism of the final report. You should research the test and interview any potential tester.

Fixing an Uneven Elementary Foundation

Try to get input from other homeschoolers about their experiences and who they have worked with. Ask your doctors about whom they would recommend.

I would recommend that you refrain from the school system testing. Why? Because they are testing for very specific reasons: school appropriate skills. The public school system is required to test your child under the current federal educational law IDEA if you request it. They must test anyone that asks to see if they need further educational assistance but be aware that each school has its own specific rules as to who gets tested. You could have trouble proving your child needs evaluation testing. Remember that each state has its own laws therefore you may or may not get assistance with your child's special needs beyond the initial testing and evaluation process. Some states are not legally obligated to assist homeschoolers in any way. Some will help. Most are in the middle and largely depend upon the current political structure of the state's educational superintendent or your county's superintendent, and in some cases your local principle has the right to deny or accept your child.

Usually homeschoolers are placed on the totem pole below the public school children, below the private schooled children, and below the early intervention children. With that many biting at the apple before you there is often little time, therapists, or money left to help your child.

You are in charge and responsible for this weighty and very important decision. There is also the very real possibility that the learning disability your child is diagnosed with is wrong or maturity inappropriate. The educational world keeps creeping up it's time table of when a child "should" know how to read, write legibly, even do higher level math. Some children are not biologically wired that fast and there is no cure but to wait and let them grow in a home that encourages and doesn't stress them about their level of learning.

"First of all, don't feel that you are stuck with a label simply because it was given to you by a school or diagnostician. There is no getting around the fact that mis-diagnoses can be made, especially if testing is not extensive enough to pick

up the differences between underachievement and true learning disabilities." — Home Schooling Children with Special Needs *by Sharon C Hensley* [1]

To pigeon hole any child/teen/adult is wrong. I have seen children blossom that had been previously written off by a professional as not educable. Each child MUST be delicately and carefully tended for as long as they need to grow and flourish. The inability to change the course a label creates in the public school system can be a major problem.

This conundrum is just as bad for a gifted child as it is for a child that is developmentally delayed. In our culture a person with above average IQ is assumed to go to college and become something big. That "big" idea can be vague and not be the passion of that child's heart but the educational machine rarely cares. They need alumni and test takers that show extraordinary results. The child's actual outcome and life become a secondary goal to what a gifted child that takes great tests can bring to the school.

Homeschooling Allows Us to Turn the Normal Education Grind on Its Head

One of the advantages of homeschooling is the fact that with a one on one relationship; we can easily see if our child isn't learning something, or worse missing the concept altogether. We can immediately stop and correct any problems and keep working until the fundamental education blocks are set.

I stay on a subject until it is mastered, not reviewed until boredom sets in. I can then be sure my child understands the foundations of learning before moving on.

Sitting around the dining room table, or at a chair near your child's desk, you will see "learning quirks" and other warning signs of disabilities because you are working with them every day. You'll see when they solve math problems incorrectly, or write their names with backwards d's. You'll notice when they have trouble sounding out words, or failing to isolate the first or last sound in a word. A quick correction and attention to persistent learning issues is much easier to deal with once you know they are there than vague behavior problems and struggling grades.

Homeschooling one child with special needs would have been daunting at one point in my life. Now I look around the dining room table at my five wonderful children all with special needs and smiles. How blessed I am!

While writing this book I had a high schooler down to a kindergartener. All were learning physical science together. This cuts down on teacher prep time, money on textbooks, workbooks, and promotes a family bonding you just can't get anywhere else. After all, when you have blown up a baking soda volcano together or picked apart an owl pellet you have some serious family memories.

As I write this the kids are going to do an egg experiment with their father. One where you put an egg into vinegar, orange juice, milk, water, salt, and soda. This experiment is perfect for the group. The littlest one will see the changes in the egg and understand it to her level of ability.

My daughter of elementary ability will be writing the science experiment out in a simplified manner.

My two at middle school levels will be writing up the experiment in a detailed manner and learning about acid verse alkaline.

My high schooler will be writing up the experiment in greater detail including things like acidity findings and critical thinking required for a well thought out hypothesis and implications of this experiment on a larger scale like will the salt in the ocean mirror the salt egg portion. Each child is learning at their level and it's not taking a huge amount of my time to plan for this science class.

When doing group subjects like this you get several perks. Like I said before you get great family time, lower cost, and less time. One of the more important side effects can be no one is singled out per grade level. I have met some very competitive kids over the years. If a younger sibling is learning material above their older sibling's grade level you hear about it. There are times that one child is advanced and shouldn't feel shame for that fact. They also shouldn't be encouraged to flaunt it in front of their siblings. I discourage competitive feuds every time because it leads to hard feelings.

Struggling Readers Are the #1 Problem in the Early Years

Did you know that Leonardo da Vinci, one of the world's most prolific artists, inventors and thinkers is thought to have been dyslexic? When he died, people entered his workrooms to categorize his materials and they thought for years he had written in code. Many years later, it was found he was not writing in code but he was writing backwards and mirror imaged like many dyslexics. Not only that but like many with dyslexia he was obviously gifted and showed strong signs of ADHD. There was journal after journal that was started but never ended. He'd just drift off to another topic. If a man hundreds of years ago with no supports or understanding of the struggles he went through could create such a wealth of invention, art, and ideas think what our children can do today!

Reading is the number one concern I hear from parents by far. When should my child know how to read? What if my preschooler is flipping letters? How do I know the difference between being young and learning and this has gone too far and is possibly a learning disability?

The first article I ever wrote to the homeschooling world was about dyslexia and our struggle with those exact questions. It was published in, "The Old Schoolhouse" magazine. Less than a week later I got a call from Ruth Beechick, a reading specialist and homeschooling advocate. She was wonderful and full of great calming information.

The first thing she did was assure me was there was a large developmentally appropriate age range for children (especially boys) to learn to read. While most children learn to read by age 7 many may not hit that maturity ability until they are 10 years old. That's normal. Remember there may be a few children who are outliers to even that age limit with no learning disability, they're just maturing later than average.

Don't get sucked into the public school mantra of "must read early." Realize that for many schools they have no choice but to try to force children as young as kindergarten to read due to testing. Homeschoolers even have to deal with testing in some states that encourage the idea we too must push our children to read early. You can get accommodations for young children if they are forced to take standardized testing. You can request an aide to read the test to your child in their early elementary years even without a known learning disability.

In "Educating the Wholehearted Child," by Clay and Sally Clarkson[2], the Clarkson's state, "Some children start reading later. Don't worry, and don't push – just keep reading aloud to them until they signal their own readiness to read (asking about words, reading signs and boxes, "reading" books). If you encounter resistance, put away the lessons until the child is ready to try again. When the time is right, the process will be natural and enjoyable. Resist the cultural pressure to be sure your child learns to read "on schedule". Your child may read much earlier or much later."

How can you homeschool a child that is not reading well or at the level of their understanding? I want you to embrace subject specific learning in this area more than any other thing you have used. Reading is part of every single subject of learning, including math. If your child is struggling with reading then it can appear that they are having problems with all subjects. This is why we have to be very deliberate with our learning materials and how we teach.

Each subject will be based not upon your child's reading ability, like most curriculum, but on the way we teach such as audio, kinetic or visual. History, science and even literature can be taught by alternative methods other than reading text. Use audio material and teach in a manner that works on visual strengths rather than relying on reading to input learning. That means you might be teaching literature by you reading out loud for years. Yes, I still read out loud to my graduated daughter when we are pouring over something she needs to know in detail. I love the teamwork. She has also found ways to learn outside the typical expected learning methods that have helped her excel well beyond her learning disability.

Along the way we have also learned some simple tweaks to our day that help. When reading material on a computer screen change the letters to a bright white and the background to a dark tone. The contrast makes it easier for a dyslexic to read. There is now a free dyslexic font that helps by taking away all the fussy little flips and makes all letters clean and clear.

There is another learning disability that often comes along with dyslexia called dysgraphia. It is a moderate to severe problem with the act of writing and seeing the written word. Many kids can fool you for a bit by drawing the letters they see but over the long term as they have to write sentences the struggle begins to show. We found that going straight to cursive helped all my kids tremendously! Whether they had a learning disability in reading or writing going to cursive helped their fine motor skills.

Another learning disability that can tag along with dyslexia or come on its own is dyscalculia. A learning disability with math and math concepts. If your child is struggling with writing numbers and lining up their problems you can simply turn your lined notebook page on its side. Voila, you have easy to see columns. You can even take a highlighter and highlight in every other column to further denote each section. Another great thing to use is graph paper. You can get graph paper that has enlarged boxes online for free, just use a search engine for graph paper. Or you can find preschool graph paper that has enlarged boxes. I take the graph paper out of the "Preschool" front cover and use it as needed. This helps your child "wrangle in pesky numbers" as one of my littles put it.

Reading is a boogie man for many homeschoolers. When it comes to reading, persistence is the key. Work on the basics, like tracking from left to right, and smooth, fluid eye movement. If necessary, think about seeing a developmental optometrist. Memorizing sight words while you are working on phonics can give your child a foundation of success to build on. Then relax and allow your child to learn reading at the pace the Lord created them too. Whether you are dealing with a learning disability or not, you and your child can find ways through, around, or over this bump in the learning road!

Teaching Two Simple Social Skills

Here is a simple method to prevent interruptions and teach manners for young children. If your child needs to get your attention and you are out and about many children with social communication issues just blurt things out. From autism to ADHD to just being a young child it happens but it's our job to teach our children that they have to wait their turn. Early in my parenting life I was taught this method of helping a child in a tangible way know that I recognize they are there but they are to wait their turn for my attention.

First, if we are out and I am talking to another adult and my child wants my attention, they put their hand on my hand or arm. I will put my hand over theirs acknowledging that I know they are there and want my attention. If the need is urgent they can tap tap my side with their hand. I would then excuse myself and find out what is wrong. Normal circumstances mean they wait their turn with my hand over theirs.

Sure there are times when the person I am talking to goes on for quite a while. If so I squeeze their hand or flash them a smile letting them know how great they are doing. At the first polite chance I have I stop and turn to my child to find out what they need me for. This simple but effective method stopped most interrupting immediately. My child needed a way to let me know they had to talk to me and they needed that hand on theirs to let them know that I was aware of their need.

Another quick parenting trick I learned with four children on the autism spectrum that had no sense of personal space: use a hula hoop! Have your child use the hula hoop to hold about at their waist level and not bump into people and things. This helps them learn the approximate space around them and others that we should politely allow. Personal space! We were blessed at a co-op to have a large group of kids join in this fun "game" during free time. I had to laugh a simple thing to most of those kids and yet they were helping my children learn personal space in such a fun way I was very grateful!

The Foundation Is Being Laid and It's Worth Taking Your Time

Our job as teachers is to build up our children and cheer them on as many tackle tough challenges. To continually be on our toes helping to seek out the best path to learning. The early elementary years have a lot of redundancy in them and homeschooling gives you extra time to get the proper therapy, tutoring or program to assist your child. Use this time to be sure the basics are understood and mastered.

I know the pressure to move on to the next skill builds quickly but you will not be helping your child to push them too fast. I have had several children that did not read until the age of 10 but when they did start reading they caught up to grade appropriate level within a year! We had another that never had to be taught how to read. We joke that she was born reading. Children are so wonderfully different in their learning abilities and disabilities. Their pace and how much they can take in and understand in a setting that we tailor to each child's learning needs.

We should be sure that our desire to keep up with the Jones doesn't snuff out the fire in our children's heart to learn. We need to foster that curiosity that young children naturally have. Cultivating a love for learning that will long outlast our homeschooling.

---

[1] Sharon C Hensley, *Home Schooling Children with Special Needs* (Redemption Press March 21, 2014)

[2] Clay and Sally Clarkson, *Educating the Wholehearted Child* (Apologia Press; 3rd edition June 15, 2011)

Chapter 8: Middle School Pressure Cooker

When did the bullying start? When was that moment when he went from the laughing kid that liked to tell jokes to the kid that was the butt of the jokes? No, that's not right. They weren't jokes. They were digs and cutting sarcasm that sliced small hurts directly to his heart.

This was not the type of "in your face" bullying like we talked about earlier that was so pronounced that you needed to remove your child from school immediately. This is the more common form of bullying. A long term low level bullying that teachers suspect, but don't see. Our children put up with it because they aren't getting physically hurt. Many think if they just keep their head down and ignore it, the bullying will go away. For months this preteen thought just that and kept trying to hold things together in school and in front of his parents. He kept thinking it will all calm down. The truth was seeping through though. His grades were plummeting and his emotions were clearly becoming gloomy and secretive.

Middle school had come and the changes both emotionally and educationally were hitting this young preteen hard. While he was beginning to experience significant bullying his learning was also suffering. His mother went to his school and talked with several of his teachers.

Being new to middle school and now spread across several teachers who all needed to have a meeting and fill out forms to decide if this was a transitioning issue or a longer term problem. Despite the fact that in elementary school, not more than 4 months earlier, his IEP team had recommended continuing supportive education assistance. For this young man the slate had been wiped clean. The idea was he could move on in his education without the "label" of special educational needs or an IEP in his record. That might work for a few who have matured to a point where they no longer needed the help or for those that could scrape by with passing grades, but this young man was not one of them. His learning disabilities were only being highlighted by the increased speed and more intense level of learning required by middle school. He was set up to fail and no one would help him or his mom until he failed out and needed an IEP.

Mom was having none of that. She had been thinking about home-schooling for years off and on but had never tried it. The day the school made it crystal clear they could do nothing for her son until after he had failed two full quarters. She decided to pull both her children out of school and began homeschooling.

Homeschooling didn't take away his learning disability or make his first day of homeschooling a fun filled joy. No. There was a struggle. He thought it was showing weakness to quit school and start learning at home. He struggled with the idea of missing his friends at school and the social activities that would come along in the next couple of years like homecoming and prom.

I was privileged to watch as this stressed and chaotic public school family slowly calmed down. Mom found her son's weaker learning points and began to focus his work to address them. Her sons began to stop the constant fighting and developed a lifelong strong relationship. The learning issues lessened as they worked and his confidence went up. Instead of a stooped, head down demeanor he began to stand up tall and look you in the eye.

This new homeschooling mom, Tracia shared with me, "I really enjoyed homeschooling and there is so much you can do with it."

The middle school jump from elementary school can be when some kids hit their stride and take off gathering awards and A's. Most kids find it's a rocky road between physical changes of the preteen years, emotional changes of the school, social cliques, and the intensity of learning accelerating all at once. Then there are a few that just do not have the tools to deal with changes that large and that quick.

There is a large jump in the number of homeschoolers during the middle school years. I believe that, like this young man and his family, the changes required of students can be too much. Many of these changes have nothing to do with learning and maturity but the pressure of middle school and its pace leaves no time for a preteen to adjust. Thankfully when you are homeschooling you can stay subject specific and try to keep the issues separate. Let your preteen deal with the emotional and physical changes normally and without intense peer scrutiny. Learning can stay on track and be dealt with like it always has been.

Helping Your Preteen Listen Not Just Hear

Preteens are very aware and delicate about your words and tone you use with them. I have found the preteen middle school years to be some of the most emotionally fraught years to deal with. It helps if you watch what you say, and how you say it before there is an issue. It's always harder to clean up a mess than to prevent one.

One of the most important tools in my kit to teach my middle schoolers is active listening. A great technique to start with middle schoolers that will help you now and most definitely in the high school years is active listening. This is a skill that is often taught in counseling (I am not a counselor FYI). I find it to be very helpful when things start to go sideways we can stop and talk through the issue

First I say, "When I told you finish up your chores, I meant all of them!" If I am saying this, I'm pretty sure I am miffed and facing the child that didn't finish their chores.

"I took out the trash!" said preteen says louder than me because she is trying to take control of the situation. But you see I know that I am the authority of the house so no matter what volume or whine level they reach I will not be pulled into the yelling game.

"Okay, we are missing something here. What do you think I asked you to do? Be very detailed." I keep that calm "I'm in control" voice going.

"You wanted the trash out of the kitchen because it was stinky." Shrug of the shoulders and a dampening of the volume. Good, we are getting to the heart of the problem.

"I asked you to finish your chores. And yes that does mean getting the stinky trash out of the kitchen but what else does it mean?"

"Oh. It means I have to take all the trash out and unload the dishwasher. Then I'm done with my chores, right?" Suddenly the light dawns that she was mad about taking trash out and I was just trying to get her to finish the rest of her chores.

This works really well for us. One of the keys here is that I have to stay in control. If I get pulled into the yelling and trying to prove to my child I'm in charge things get out of hand. Know that you are in charge and the authority of the house. That will destress you and by doing so make the whole situation much easier.

Active listening is also repeating, in your own words, what the person you are talking with just said.

I say, "You need to finish up the math problem. Then we are going to grandmas for dinner."

Your child repeats what they hear. Be aware this can get hilarious at times and at other times I am left scratching my head trying to figure out how they possibly got that out of what I said!

Child repeats, "I have to finish math. Then we are going to grandma's to have that stinky broccoli bake again." Sigh and huff. That is a preteen, people, get used to it.

Knitting Together a Strong Family

Is your family drifting apart as your child becomes a preteen? A family dealing with special needs can find itself under strain and attack in these middle years. You have to be proactive and fight for your family and its continued cohesion. Homeschooling is not only a learning opportunity that will remove stumbling blocks, frustrating environments, and help strengthen your family ties. Homeschooling is a family learning journey.

Middle School Pressure Cooker

I have talked with many families that pulled their children from school because their teens were becoming strangers. You aren't alone nor are you being selfish in making the decision to bring a preteen home to be sure they keep healthy priorities and strengthen your family ties. You only get a chance at this once. Homeschooling will be different though and many teens buck the system at first.

Children that went to school were bombarded with tons of sensory input. Visually lots of different items on walls from lockers to posters. Smells, good and bad, permeate the school. Children jostling each other constantly to go in and out of rooms. The entire school building is a nightmare to a sensory intense child or an anxious child. It is full of unexpected input.

Even though it would seem all teens would want to come home given those odds stacked against them it is not uncommon to have a teen yearning for the chaos. It is not because the chaos of middle school was healthy or helpful for them. It's often because, well face it, they're teens and in the middle of hormonal chaos.

"But MOMMMMM I want to go back and go to the winter dance!" Kids are full of wants. What does our child need? It is our job to decide what is in their best interest. Sometimes a firm "no", is the best and only decision for our preteen.

There is always a "grass is greener" mentality. Children need to be taught to be content. They are not born with contentment. It is a learned trait.

At home we are able to provide a structure and sameness that many of our children need. Then we can choose opportunities that would best provide our child with success. I do not believe that our children have to be awash in other kids to be able to learn proper social skills. Isn't that the basis of the book "The Lord of the Flies"? Instead we should be aiming at successful, real relationships. Keep the big picture in mind. We teach our children not just for this one year of their life. We teach for a lifetime, so that their adulthood will be more successful and filled with happiness.

Gifted Learners Diverge

In the early years of elementary life, it can be easy to let a gifted learner just follow their interests. Homeschoolers have no reason to be constrained by grade level books. We can just keep going further in depth with a topic your child loves or higher in grade level to keep your gifted child challenged and engaged in learning. For many with higher intelligences there is no stopping their thirst for learning.

Jennifer, a homeschooling mom of a gifted child told me, "As a gifted child, my son doesn't often need much sleep, so he often does his independent work in the wee hours when I'm sleeping. This might include DVDs (he's been known to watch Dave Ramsey at 3am), audio books, working on projects or (non-dangerous) experiments, or art work."

The middle school years often highlight how much further ahead academically your child is than their peers. However it that can have the opposite affect because emotionally they may be closer to their age range. The balance of a high IQ and being 11 is tough.

Homeschooling lets us be subject specific even with gifted learners. Gifted learners are notorious for being asynchronous in their learning. Their writing can be so delayed compared to their intellectual level they have dysgraphia. However their math is so far ahead that you have to find outside means to teach them more because your child who's in the 7th grade, is on a higher math level than you. That's okay! In fact, no, that's great!

You can find online classes for your child to take. You can even enroll your child in college classes where they can start earning college credits while helping your gifted learner keep stretching their limits and learning more and more. The pressure on you will lessen if you share the responsibility with an online program. If there are subjects you aren't familiar with, try finding a mentor for your child at a nearby university.

While making sure your child's emotional and social needs are met we can also ensure they excel academically. We go to church and have a wonderful group of friends. There are various groups such as the American Heritage Girls; Boy Scouts; martial arts leagues and many more opportunities that you will have time for because of the flexibility of your homeschooling schedule. There are a group of highly intelligent children that are extremely gifted. They can have serious problems fitting into groups because they are so advanced. Often if you find groups that are focused on a specific things such as saving sea turtles where the focus of every one is on saving turtles your child may fit in better than if it is a group of similar aged peers.

HOW TO ADDRESS AND WORK THROUGH OBSESSIVE-COMPULSIVE DISORDER

My daughter has autism and had showed some lingering signs of obsessional habits. Through her early years they came and went but never quite went away 100%. As the preteen years approached things started to get more intense which is common. My daughter showed signs of OCD (Obsessive-compulsive disorder) in her early preteen years.

Her OCD would be rather benign except for the one strange place she felt the urge to repeat it: the parking lot. My daughter felt the need to run her finger over any sign that is indented or bumped out. She had to run her finger along the beveled letters and numbers on a license plate. That meant she would be squatting down behind a car or van running her finger over the license. If the driver didn't notice or we weren't on the lookout all the time she could have been hurt by someone backing out. After talking with the doctor he gave us this great way to tackle her OCD behavior.
(overleaf)

Steps to Help You Conquer OCD Behaviors:

Get eye to eye – Get down on your child's level. Engage them both with speech and physically BE there next to them in the moment.

Engage in the act (if safe or possible) – Obsessive-compulsive disorder is a mental loop that is supremely important to the person experiencing it, especially when they are in the middle of the loop. You need to let your child know that you feel it is important as well. Ask what they feel like while they are completing their looping behavior. You need to know what is going through their mind so you can pinpoint exactly how to help them stop.

I would take my hand and gently put it over my daughter's hand. Then we would outline several letters together while talking. She opened up more when I was doing this then when I just crouched down beside her. She needed to know I was not shaming her or angry but I really wanted to know what was going through her mind at that moment.

Find an end point to the obsessional thought loop – This where it gets tricky. Look for a natural conclusion to their loop and pull them out at that moment. You are showing and practicing how to end the OCD in a healthy manner. You are helping to replace the unhealthy loops.

Now to end the loop in a healthy manner, I had to start by ending the loop at the end of the license or word if she was outlining a sign. When I first started this technique she would not stop during a word. She was even resistant to stopping in the middle of a sentence if it was a sign. There were times I had to give her a deep hug and use that hug to guide her away to the van or store to get her away from the OCD temptation and yes there were times she screamed. As we continued to be patient and persistent with her I was then able to stop in the middle of the sentence at the end of a word. Finally I could stop her at the end of a letter!

Replace with appropriate action – Now it is time to put in place something else that will healthfully distract your child. Don't give them tech if you aren't willing to allow tech to become an OCD stand in. Don't give gum if you aren't able to have it when needed during OCD loops. You might think those ideas are just plain crazy so why even suggest them but like every other child or family we have talked about in this book each child is absolutely wonderfully unique and in desperate need of individual care. While tech would never by my first attempt as a distraction I have used it when meltdown and or self-destructive behavior were the alternative I saw my child starting. I would rather have my child play a limited amount of time on tech than hurt themselves. Try again next time to stop the behavior before it gets that far.

Some great first level distractions in life or during homeschooling behavior should be singular. Meaning it should not involve other people or be distracting to others. This will help keep your child's behavior as a private issue. If you are homeschooling with other kids at the table it will help from distracting their learning.

My daughter is currently working on self-regulating this behavior. Some people need medications to help them learn self-regulation and prevent the biochemical issues that OCD triggers. The goal is to teach our child how to deal with their OCD themselves so as they grow into adults they will live a healthier independent life.

In second level distractions mom, dad, or a favorite piece of tech is involved. Things are starting to fray at the edges and you can see that a meltdown is on the way. You need to jump in and firmly distract from the coming storm. If the situation calls for it feel no shame or guilt in pulling out the iPad. There are lots of great apps that can be safe, learning, and calming for kids/preteens/teens that are looping and need an engaging distraction.

My goal is to use a simple phrase or reminder to get her back to dealing with the OCD herself and self-regulating. There are bad days though and we need to be prepared for them. OCD is not an issue that is going to go away easily. For some they will always have to deal with it and the siren's call of the mental loops like stimming in autism. It can be a craving that we have to support our children's battle against.

Finally you need to remove your child from the OCD issue if you can. You must get help. It is time for medication. Picking fingers till they bleed cannot continue there are several health concerns there. Pulling hair until you have balding patches is not healthy and could be a social issue for your growing child. Looping so badly in their conversations or activities that they cannot have a successful conversation at a party or co-op class has to be addressed at a professional level.

Mental Health Issues Can Show Themselves in the Early Teen Years

The pre-teen, and teenage years are a common time for mental illnesses such as: depression, anxiety, Bi Polar, eating disorders and many more to show themselves. I am not a counselor. I do know through my family's experiences and interaction with hundreds of families across the country that mental illness is in homeschooling community, just as it is in public schooling community. Homeschooling doesn't cause mental illness but I believe that it can help us address and support our child as they deal with it more effectively.

I am not a big fan of treatments given by big mental health hospitals. Why? Because the several large mental health hospitals that I have had contact with were extremely overwhelmed with month's long waiting lists for treatment group and individual sessions. Thus some doctors reverted to medicating heavily so the person didn't hurt themselves, with the assumption they will work on the problem over the years. I can understand not wanting a person to hurt themselves but many of these medications can cause problems that are just as egregious. One size treatment does not fit all.

I am not denouncing all medications for mental illness. No. There are times long term and short that medications are the difference between a functioning individual and one that cannot. I also encourage that whether it's a medication for bi-polar disorder or ADHD. Use the assistance of the medication to put into place better coping skills and an understanding of what you are dealing with. Then if possible lower the level of the medication.

We had a period of time when a mediation was needed to help stop self-injurious behavior after a stroke caused a surge in behavioral issues. I am sorry, but I kept it a secret. The behaviors were pronounced and easy to see but it was more acceptable to just shrug it off as an autism problem. We had already lost so many friends I was afraid that the friends we had left would see a mental illness as a personal parenting problem or that my child is some way was causing the problem. I was wrong!

I will never hide my child's illness for personal or social reasons. As caretaker to my child's tender soul I will watch carefully to not share information that my child doesn't want the world to know. I want you to know that you didn't cause your child's mental illness and neither did they. Families dealing with mental health problems need support. Dear friends dealing with this today you are fighting a hard fight but you are not alone.

Mental Illness Doesn't Care If You Are Homeschooling or Not

"I hate myself!" I heard this and my mother's heart broke. I didn't understand why my child was so incredibly upset, frustrated, and removed from me. My child didn't either, they wanted to be happy but they just couldn't.

Depression is not a condition only for adults or even teens. Children can become depressed. We are not talking just sad and upset because they didn't go to the movies. I am talking terribly, heart wrenchingly blue. When my child said they hated themselves they were under their bed crying. My child was 7 years old that day and devastatingly sad.

If you suspect there is a problem, talk to your child. You may want to talk with your child's pediatrician. You may even want to have an evaluation with a mental health professional a psychologist or psychiatrist.

SIGNS TO LOOK FOR

- Change in appetite, sleep, or activity

- Less playing with others, tending to remain apart more

- More aggressive outbursts and frustrations that are unfounded

- Headaches, stomach aches, vague problems that linger

- Hurting themselves

- Sadness: they lose that sparkle and laughter

- Suicidal thoughts *please take any suicidal thought seriously*

Please keep in mind you have not failed as a parent if your child is depressed. Depression is caused by a huge number of things including hormonal changes, medications, genetics, emotional stress (such as a loved one passes away, or parents' divorce). What is needed is a focus on healing and staying healthy.

Depression is a serious issue but not a life stopping one. We can work with our wonderful children and help them recapture the smiles and laughter. This is not an easy one stop journey. Being aware and actively working to fight depression has helped us tremendously!

Middle School Can Become the Beginning of a Wonderful Independent Life for Your Child

The march towards independence with your child, as they are able, has begun. Start incorporating them into their curriculum decision, scheduling times, and general path of their education.

Higher faster education such as Algebra 1 is now normal for 8th grade. Your teen may not be there yet and there is no harm waiting. Many teens don't settle into their more critical, logical, independent thinking until their high school years. This push to make teens take bigger and more intense leaps into their "college preparation" could actually be cutting out a whole section of teens that could be college worthy, just not mature enough physically or emotionally for the intense level of learning required at such a young age.

Homeschooling is a great fit whether you are dealing with a physical disability or a mental health issue. Don't be afraid to reach out and create a life that is safe, enriched, and allows the help needed to get through these problem as a strong family!

Chapter 9: High School and Beyond!

Panic stricken? Ah, you must be the parent of a high schooler. The most panic stricken point of homeschooling for me was realizing in my state this was it. It was the cliff I was either going to step off of and keep homeschooling or stop and put my teen into the local high school. From the beginning of the freshman year on any credits and classes she took would not be credited towards her graduation. That meant if she decided as a junior she wanted to go to high school she would have to take make up courses, even summer school for all the "missed" classes. Just to make things even more uncomfortable there is no testing out, even AP (advanced placement) or CLEP (college level entrance placement) testing would not be accepted. It was the last trick in the bag for the public school system to get my daughter back into their rank and file.

Relax my friend you can do this! Many parents have already traveled this path and quite successfully. I have walked down this path myself. Whether you are new or a homeschooling veteran, facing freshman year of high school is scary. All those reasons you chose to start home-schooling now seem so small next to a diploma, college education, or joining the military. Can I as a mere mom truly provide a high quality education that will allow my child to make it in the world? How can I teach my teen things like higher level math and a foreign language?

High school, like every other year, will have its special ups and downs. We are going to need to do more paperwork in high school, even if your state doesn't require it. You will need paperwork for your teen's diploma and college requirements such as a transcript. You will need to prove to others that your teen had a full education and is qualified for college, military, other schools or employment. You will also need paperwork to show that you are continuing to engage, educate, and enrich your moderately or severely affected teen in cases where you will need to have legal guardianship.

Out of all the grades the high school years are really where we have to make some large decisions based on our teen's strengths and weaknesses. Can my teen make decisions for themself? Can they learn to live on their own? Will they need care all their life? Will my teen be able to read well enough to make it through college? While I understand that we need to be thinking ahead, never let this forward thinking deny our child from changing course if they choose. After all, the goal of homeschooling is to have an independent thinker and adult as prepared as they are able for life.

Tell Me Straight About Graduation!

Graduation and diplomas are considered the pinnacle of the learning experience. Just the thought of diplomas, college entrance requirements and where to go when your teen becomes an adult can leave you in a cold sweat. Take a deep breath. You have faced every obstacle so far and made it. Your family is facing high school and you have almost successfully navigated the whole educational process at home. You can successfully navigate the finally years of official homeschooling!

As special needs homeschoolers we are looking at several angles. From my daughter that is gifted and more advanced than, in comparison to others her age, to another teen that is struggling mightily with the basics of a high school education. You can homeschool all the way through high school. There are various levels of diplomas and educational completion. In high school there are also many other paths you can successfully and legally take to help your teen blossom into a godly productive adult.

Let's start with the end in mind so you don't have to sit and worry about it the whole chapter. The number one question I get from those that are transitioning into high school or thinking about bringing their child home from high school is "what about graduation?"

When Does a Special Needs Homeschooler Graduate?

What does a special needs homeschooler do when their teen turns 18? or 21? What does a teen need to know to get a diploma? Who gives my teen a diploma? My teen is chronologically of age but not in ability, are there options for us? What do I do now that we have reached the end of our journey?

Each state is different and thus they all have slightly different versions of what a teen must know to be considered acceptable for graduation. Look at your homeschooling law first. Is there anything in the law specifically about graduation? Is there just an age range you must register your child until? You must first meet or exceed your state's law. Most states do not have a mandate specifying what is acceptable for graduation for homeschoolers.

A diploma is simply a professional looking paper that states your teen has successfully completed a high school level course of study. It is perfectly acceptable for you, the home schooling parent, to issue that diploma! There is nothing special about a public school diploma. High schools like to crow about accreditation. What is sad is a high percentage of schools across the US are not accredited.

Homeschoolers tend to issue parent signed diplomas. You can have an umbrella school, cyber school, or distance learning school issue a diploma. Personally if hubby and I are hanging in there for 12 years of homeschooling I am going all the way and issuing a diploma!

DIPLOMA OPTIONS

Honors or college preparatory level diplomas will require a higher GPA and the basic classes to match college entrance requirements (such as two years of a foreign language, higher level math, AP classes, or even some dual enrollment college classes).

The standard level diploma can be for any child that has passed the high school level.

An occupational diploma is for a teen that is ready for the workforce but did not excel at academics. There is even an option for teens that are not intellectually able to pass a high school level program to receive a letter of completion.

You can issue a letter of completion. This means that your child was not academically able to graduate. This is not failure! A teen's abilities and how far they can go are not a reflection of you. You can rest assured that your diligent training, homeschooling, and loving of your child is exactly what they needed!

Why would you issue a letter of completion? You would need to for legal purposes, such as when you petition the court to become legal guardian, they are going to want to know that you are caring for your teen. If you teen receives Social Security Disability payments that is a paper they like to have. It is something to be proud of. You have kept going and you and your teen should be just as happy about this as anyone else receiving a diploma.

Transcripts: How to Get From Freshman to Graduate!

You will need to fill out a transcript of your teen's classes and credit from the time they began taking high school level work. That will mean 8th grade level work for some teens, for others that will be freshman and beyond. You will want to have the title of the course and a description of the course taken. Keep it simple and mimic your local high school's courses so that when the local college reads your transcript they have a good understanding of what you are talking about.

What if your child can't take a required class like Physical Education? You will need to adjust or modify the course as per your teen's ability. This is perfectly reasonable given if your teen were in high school they would adjust the curriculum as well to fit your teen's needs. Don't be afraid to tweak courses to accommodate for your teen's special need.

High School and Beyond!

Most of the top colleges are happy to take homeschooled students that show a transcript and usually one of the big tests, such as ACT or SAT. There is a recent trend towards allowing in students that don't take the high stakes testing but do come to the college and request entrance, much like a job interview, in place of or along with the college's placement testing. I love this new approach because it is so much more personal. Allowing both the college and your teen to get to know each other better.

High Stakes Testing for College

High stakes testing is a must for most colleges. There has been a recent movement towards colleges not requiring an ACT or SAT test score but over all you will need to take one of these two tests. For those with a learning disability you can get accommodation for these tests.

First and most important you have to be in touch with the testing proctors at the very least six weeks ahead of time. They have to know and possibly hire an aide to help your teen with the test. You want to give them time and all paperwork they request promptly. Remember it is always a good idea to have the test givers in a good mood when they see your teen, not annoyed.

You will need to have the learning disability or medical issue documented by the appropriate doctor and it will have to fall under specific allowable disabilities by the College Board or test your teen will be taking.

Here are some accommodation you can ask for – this list is not all encompassing:

- Extra time

- Larger print for testing material

- For those with ADHD or sensory issues you might get short breaks throughout the testing.

- If you have dysgraphia or other writing problems you may be given a computer or other means to type your answers rather than write them.

Teflon Learners Need a Big Dream

Do you have a dawdler in the house? The one that shows up late every single day and yet the commute is about 10 feet from the couch? Or they are there but checking email and social updates until they are reminded there is no tech at the table. The eyes roll and they fold their arms and slump down into the chair to glare at you for bothering them. You teach your teen what equivalent fractions are for the 5th time and they still look at you with the dull, "huh?" look plastered all over their face. Sorry but you may have a Teflon learner on your hands.

No matter how much education you scoop into that brain pan it's going to slide right out the minute you stop talking or the test is over. Why? This is so frustrating you have taken a long time to pull together just the right learning material and plan out the lessons. They are getting nothing from homeschooling. Is it you?

Probably not. Teenagers love to push the limits of authority. They are learning and understanding so much more in these few short teen years than ever before and you are the one person they know without a doubt will always be there for them. That often means you are the brunt of their desire to see how far they can go. Parents of children they adopted or are fostering will know this type of defiance.

How can we help our teen get back on track and not let them take over homeschooling? We are going to give them the independence they are craving but in a healthy methodical way. Do you remember the big dream of what your child would grow up to be and what great achievements they would attain? Now it's time for your teen to step up to the plate and take responsibility of their own life and big dream. They get to define their own future with our experience to help guide them.

It is time to create a motivation for *why* our teens should put effort into their high school education above and beyond the simple churning hrough to get a diploma. Our teens need specific goals instead of a wide march towards a nebulous goal of "adulthood".

I talked with a group of teens that were beginning to get into trouble and drift from their higher grades to just making it through. Most were public schooled but a couple were in and out of homeschooling. The general consensus from the group about why they were all struggling in life and education was who cares if we get a diploma at the local technical college they take anyone.

I asked them, "What will you guys be doing in ten years when you are about thirty."

Lots of laughter. No one had thought about when they get old. I persisted, "What about a family? Anyone want to get married and have kids?"

Everyone wanted to find the perfect woman and have a family.

"Okay so how will you take care of that family?"

When I began drilling down to specifics of how they would pay for a house, get good insurance so their lovely wife could have prenatal care for their little bundle of joy. I started to get very uncomfortable looks. They just hadn't thought about it that way. They were all just churning through to get a diploma and become an adult!

We need to help them identify their goals, so they can develop a plan for that job, or apartment of their own. When you have renewed your teen's reason to learn, often they stop being a Teflon learner and they participate. Get the local paper and look at exactly what an apartment would cost and show your child the utility bills. We aren't trying to scare them about adulthood we are teaching them. Teach them about credit, how to balance a check book or how online banking works. If we don't teach our teens they will learn the hard way and no one wants that.

At Risk Teens

Teens with learning disabilities and other special needs are an "at risk" category. They are more likely to take part in risky behavior and less likely to fully understand the outcome of that behavior. In this world of social media and interconnectedness our teens are more open to strangers then they have ever been. This could develop into a dangerous situation.

Also teens with learning disabilities are used to failure so they begin incorporating that into their general manner. Failure feeds on itself creating a depressed, anxious teen making it harder for them to succeed the next time. Our job as parents is to show our children that taking responsibility and control of the situation is the best solution. Homeschooling will allow you to immediately address those feelings of failure and stop the self-destructive cycle.

We may also have to address behaviors for biological reasons. Teens with ADHD are more prone to risky less thoughtful behavior. As parents we will need to help our teens develop a plan to overcome their natural inclination to just DO. We have a wait and see period of 48 hours on big decisions or buys in the house. This helps our teen to get out of the frenzy of the moment and calmly think and pray about the next step. If she still wants to buy the item after 48 hours then she can. This 48 hour cooling off period has been a wonderful tool to direct and keep our teen focused.

One way to help our teens and stop them from making errors in judgement is to begin early, teaching them not just the rules of your home and the laws of the land but the whys are often just as important. Drugs are illegal because they lead to addiction, extreme behavior, injury, and death. That clarifies to your teen that you are not just using your power as a parent but thoughtfully deciding the rules of your house for the good of all.

Your Awesome Teen Wants to Come Home and Homeschool!

Usually it's the parents that make the decision to homeschool, there is a growing movement of high schoolers asking their parents if they can come home to homeschool. A high schooler has a unique opportunity to be old enough that parents don't necessarily have to be home during the day. I know families that are in constant contact with their teen but their teen is home learning via online programs while the parents work.

A new high schooler turned homeschooler told me, "Learning is easier at my own pace but I'm learning more. It's not as hard as people make it out to be."

Teens can come home from high school and excel in homeschooling! They can learn more in depth in the subjects they love. You can take two sciences in one year if that is what you love! You can catch up in math or take foreign language that your school didn't offer but you goal is go live there. I have children who have or are learning Chinese, French, Japanese, and Italian (more to come I am sure).

Mom don't be afraid of subjects that are above your head or algebra that is hard to remember. You have teacher's books that can guide you through. There are online options. You can even get DVD lessons to guide your teen through upper level education. Now fabulous colleges and universities like MIT are allowing free online courses. Let's not forget the very popular KHAN and STEM programs. Do remember that you are dealing with adult level learning and teaching for many of these options and you have a teen. It's still a reasonable parenting decision to watch these educational videos first.

Military and Homeschooling, Oil and Water?

Can my teen with a learning disability still get in the military like they dream? That answer is changing for the better! Check the law as of today for the answer. HSLDA is well updated on military and homeschooling issues. Homeschoolers are now considered first tier applicants, as though they had gone to a fully accredited high school That will get your foot in the door then your teen will need to take the ASVAB (Armed Services Vocational Aptitude Battery) test of general skill, test taking ability, and knowledge of a wide variety of topics. Having taken this test to get into the Navy I can give you a heads up. My husband and I both went to our Navy recruiter, before we met, and talked about joining up. Each recruiter started some paperwork for us but right there and then with no previous notice set us in a quiet room with the ASVAB test and had us take it. It was a general knowledge test and the timing for it was generous. This test was not as intense as the ACT, SAT or PSAT.

If your young adult wishes to be in the military there is a now a better chance they can. Check the regulations on homeschooling through the DOD (Department of Defense). If you have problems having your diploma accepted or being forced to take a GED remember homeschoolers are considered 1st tier. This is very important and should stop a recruiter from forcing additional wait times or testing.

The ASVAB test will clearly show if you qualify and for what level of job the military has. You can have ADHD or eye issues now and still qualify under certain regulations. Don't take a "no" from your recruiter to be the end of the conversation. Most recruiters I know are excited to include homeschoolers. There are still some that either have not been trained enough or have a personal reasons against homeschooling. The good thing is in the military there is a clear chain of command and you can always go to the next person up the chain of command for clarification or to override the recruiter's judgment.

I met my husband in the Navy. I don't regret a moment of that wonderful time. If you have the desire and ability to be in the military go for it!

Alternatives to College

Eighteen is not a magic number. There is no guarantee that our teens are going to be ready or willing to fly the coop at that precise moment. Most states allow you to keep schooling your child until they are twenty-one. This can be helpful when you need to keep them on your health insurance, or SSDI, or you need to seek legal guardianship to keep your young adult safe.

It's not a topic many like to talk about but this is a very real problem. A teen that can learn material but not make common sense decisions. A teen that sees others their age going off on their own or making decisions about life can become rebellious. As parents, you need to have clear reasons as to why your child with a disability can or cannot transition to a life without supervision.

There are assisted living homes. As a homeschooler I don't feel right with that decision. I would rather create an apartment over my garage so my semi-independent child can have some space and learn the skills needed for living independently. Or for my teen that is going to grow into an adult that cannot live on their own, that's okay too. I will keep homeschooling and parenting as I have done since they were born.

For kids that are able to spread their wings and try college or a job on their own, be choosy. Marshal University here in West Virginia has an Asperger's track that pairs freshmen with Asperger's with an older student that has been trained to help introduce them to the campus and friends over the course of a semester. Colleges are catching on to the trend of assisting in a long term way helping teens to settle into college. I LOVE it! Good job colleges!

Finding a trade and interning is also a great possibility. Baking, wood working, computer repair or as available you can find one time jobs online: such as editing an article and you get paid for that article. These short term projects can keep the stress down and there is a clearly defined beginning and end to the project.

My graduated teen has chosen to take a year off. We set up rules that she needs to be productive in some manner. She has rules to follow living under my roof just like she always has but with the independence of an adult. Her health greatly restricts what she is able to do for a job so as part of her final semester in high school we sought out a business curriculum so that she could run her own business from home if she chose. I believe that it is my duty as homeschooling parent, teacher and guide to open every possible avenue for my young adult's future It's up to them to choose which they will follow – writing, at home jobs or service projects like with our local no-kill shelter. The online world has opened all sorts of avenues to be creative, working, and adding to your community and family. Everything from a freelance job as a writer, art design, to a social media director. For those less able there are great places to create handmade items and sell them such as Etsy. While this may not be a source of income it can be a source of pride, accomplishment and can create self-confidence.

Homeschooling for Life

Our goal is to raise up kids that can interact and be able to handle the world. It may take our special young adults a year or two more training and guidance then the average child. Protecting your child is not smothering them. It is assuring that they have the space and time to mature on God's time table not an education chart on the wall in the teacher's lounge.

I accept that my teen is a wonderful person. I long ago realized that a person turning into an adult at the age of 18 was just a piece of paper. My beautiful child may never be able to make those adult decisions. If that happens then neither of us have failed. We will just keep going. My responsibility as a parent doesn't stop at any certain age.

For these reasons and many more I will guard my child's heart and soul as long as it is my responsibility. I will protect and shelter my special child as they long as they need it. Their mental abilities may not match their physical age. I will watch and guard their hearts as zealously as I guard their mind and body. I am a parent of a special needs child I can stand up under intense pressure.

No matter the path your family takes while helping your child with autism don't be afraid to be different. Don't be afraid to think out of the box. Some teens will grow up and leave the nest others will not. This is a very personal decision based on facts that only you and your child's doctors know. Don't let the world bully you into thinking your child *has* to become independent at a specific time. You are the parent. You know your child the best. Give your teen the freedom to succeed to the best of their ability!

Dear mom that has never heard a word uttered by your child. You are strong and have long ago learned that life with your child, now young adult is how it will be. I want to encourage you to keep the big dream. You will one day hear your child praise you to the Lord. That will be a fine day when your hard work. The days and nights of endless care, changes, hospital stays will all be brought before the Lord and your child will see, know, and tell the Lord what a great parent you are. Keep strong my friend you are my hero.

What a Grand Adventure!

Who knew the teen years would be so stressful and yet such a delight? The balance is swinging towards independence for most teens now. Are they ready? Can they make it on their own? What do I do if I run out of educational time and my child still doesn't know enough? Homeschooling through the teen years is different, but no harder than the early years. You bucked the system then, just keep going now!

High school is going to require a certain amount of specific paperwork and attention to subject details that you may not have had to deal with previous to this. The goal at the end of high school is a diploma. That means you need to attain a set level of educational experience.

There are also many of our teens that are aiming for college, military, or internships that require a high level of academic achievement. We start that journey in 8th grade year. Planning a path to get from here to there.

There is no reason to be upset if you have started looking into this later then 8th grade. We can get to the ultimate goal of graduation together! I assure you that homeschooling your child will not prevent them from getting a diploma nor from going to the majority of colleges.

Homeschooling When Learning Isn't Easy

Homeschooling is absolutely possible and responsible method of educating your child! I have loved parenting teens. Over the teen years for most of my children I have become more of a guide and less of a teacher. Turning the decision making slowly over to them as they are able. The end of senior year came with fanfare and joy for the whole family. Homeschooling all the way through was a success!

You can enjoy that success as well!

Chapter 10: Stressed and Locked in the Bathroom

"**Y**ou didn't *say* we had to do math today, so I'm not doing it!" came the strident voice of my son. He was refusing to work on his math lesson for the day. It was the last subject he needed to do before he was free to go and play. If he would just buckle down and work he could be all done in less than half an hour.

Frankly my son had me on a technicality. I had not said math that morning when asked exactly what did he had to do that day. However math is a subject that is covered every day and is on the daily schedule on the wall for every day. He couldn't wiggle out of the fact that every other day of the year we work on math. He was going to have to complete his assignment before he could go watch TV or play a computer game.

I started with common sense and reasoning, "You know we have math every day. You need to stop arguing and finish the assignment."

"You didn't say math and I'm not doing it!" His arms were crossed. He was craning his head hard to the left to stare at the wall and not the math workbook or me. Shaking his head muttering "you didn't say I had to do it this morning," He was starting to settle into a mental loop. We had to find a way to stop this immediately!

I tried to engage him and help walk him through the OCD loop. Nope. Distraction didn't work either. I tried everything in my bag of tricks but this situation just deteriorated into a standoff.

This was a delicate situation where he was being rebellious but he was also dealing with a very real mental issue that he needed compassion for. I needed to remain in charge and the authority for our entire homeschool. I had a table full of little ones watching and whether they knew it or not deciding if it was time for them to create a fuss and get out of work themselves. We needed to find some breathing room and balance. Frustration and anger were beginning to color both my son and my view of the situation.

I told my son to go to his room and cool down for ten minutes. Then I excused myself from the table and did what any mother that is up to her eyeballs in frustration with few places to truly be alone when you have five young kids. I went to my private get-away, the bathroom.

I went to the bathroom to cool down myself. I was vigorously cleaning the faucet into a high gloss shine when I heard the door being jiggled.

Exasperation dripping from every syllable, "Oh come on, can't I have a moment's peace?"

I turned around to see which child was trying to get in and saw a gray cat's paw under the door playing with a loose yarn from the carpet. I had to laugh.

God knows how to help me reduce frustration and stress. I returned to the table and homeschooling with a smile. When 10 minutes were up my son returned and without another argument he finished his math.

Things worked out so great because we had been down this path many times before and we had a plan. Even in his rebellious state my son knew that he needed to self-regulate and calm himself. When he was calm like me he knew it was time to get back to work.

When my children were young and their sensory needs were at their peak, my husband and I had little idea what was going on and we were stressed! Not just a little stressed but stretched to a point where at times I felt just one more drop of trouble would break us.

I can remember calling my husband, at his job, from the bathroom crying over what I thought was my bad parenting. My husband was trying to calm me down.

Stressed and Locked in the Bathroom

I had children that would not look me in the eye or respond to my questions. We were constantly staying at home because going out meant we were most likely facing a major meltdown in public. I was trapped at home with lovely but incredibly needy children. I was starting to wear down.

Just a few short years earlier while locked in the bathroom after another similar issue I hit my lowest point. It felt like chaos was overwhelming me, my family, and our homeschooling. That night my husband and I talked about what all was happening in the family and how to correct it. We realized that a dear friend of ours had been encouraging us to get two of our children evaluated for autism. The more we read about autism the more plausible the diagnosis seemed. Working together and making a plan to move forward helped relieve the pressure that had been building. It restored my inner calm and my ability to deal with our children in a healthier way.

Soon after that two of our children were diagnosed with autism. A week after that some testing came in that eventually lead to the diagnosis of our genetic disease. That bottoming out in the bathroom just begging for a few moments calm had to happen. My husband and I needed to see how strained we were. We needed to see, as a couple and as parents, how frustrating and stressed our lives had become in order to correct our course as a family and learn to thrive.

Knowing you have a problem helps but that's not the whole solution. Just knowing that our child had autism didn't take away the frustration and stress that built up every day, but becoming educated on autism and the why's behind my children's behavior did help. Having a structure and plan in place when things began to go wrong also helped alleviate stress.

A Truths Homeschooling Mom's Need to Know

The biggest truth you need to know, especially if your child has a medical condition or learning disability, is *you are not your child's grade or ability*. Your worth is not attached to your child's ability to overcome dyslexia, or some number on a standardized test. Most of us see how these artificial means of quantifying our children are not a true picture of our child and yet I see moms using those same numbers to condemn themselves as poor teachers or too lax with their lesson plans.

Another trap many of us fall into is we aren't progressing at the dreamed of pace back before you started the year. The pace you wanted to set so your child could make up the two years difference his parting IEP highlighted. You cannot make your child learn or even learn at the pace you desire. We are homeschooling because we realize that our unique learners need space and time to mature. They are learning at the pace the Lord has intended and we need to listen to that or you are going to land in a daily struggle with frustration with yourself or your child.

Let me share with you the truth behind burnout: it's the fine line between Expectation and Reality. When the homeschooling starts we all have high hopes, lots of plans, and ideas to fill a year. Then along comes reality. Medical issues crop up, money issues happen, your child is struggling with one of the basic concepts of math, or your child is just having a grumpy time changing to homeschooling. All these things and more can happen to derail a perfectly normal homeschooling family. Now throw in the fact that we are special needs families and start with many of those extra pressures. Reality can burn our lesson book to smithereens and frazzle our nerves in a few short months.

How do you pull back from burnout and giving up homeschooling? First, let us realize that we need to stop making our own life harder. Stop pouring out so much of yourself that you forget who you are. When is the last time you read a book, or drew a picture, or took a walk by yourself to just enjoy the breeze? If you can't answer that question then it has been MUCH too long. Find a person to help you by taking the responsibility of your children off your hands totally so you can go take a walk, read a book, get a coffee with your best friend.

Now let's get our expectations of homeschooling back on track. I find taking a once a month in-service day is very helpful. That day I make sure that I have worksheets put away in an orderly manner. I double check each child's learning progress and tweak their learning material if I need to. This is also a great time to go online and find a unit study that enhances the history lessons we are doing. Find extra experiments that we can do. This day is dedicated to realigning what is happening in our daily life and what my lesson plan is dreaming up. So that reality and my high expectations don't wreck our homeschooling.

In-service days and Sunday night's when I go over our homeschooling are great times to check the pace of our homeschooling. Each child will learn at their own pace but if your textbook is slowing them down your child will get grumpy. This will create a homeschooling atmosphere that annoys everyone at the table. My daughter with dyslexia was behind in learning phonics. When she began falling behind in math I thought it was related to her dyslexia and so I just urged her to do more practice. I slowed down to work more and added things like flashcards and extra worksheets. Again and again we would meet in the morning and by late afternoon this elementary student was the only one still at the table with the math workbook open grinding her teeth. This was not how I envisioned homeschooling.

One day while reassessing her over all work I noticed that in other areas like science she was doing math at or above the lessons in her math workbook. I tried something out of the box the next day. My daughter grumped in and sat next to me knowing that math was the first subject. I opened her book.

"Okay so last week you were doing this page. It stunk, didn't it." I told my daughter in a matter of fact tone.

My daughter looked at me like "what is wrong with my mom?" but there was a glimmer of hope. Frankly I think she was hoping I would ditch all math forever but that wasn't in the plans. I did have another interesting idea.

"Today you are going to have the option to finish this lesson, OR skip to the back of the math workbook (easily 40 pages further on) and do your best on the final page."

The whole table of kids thought I had lost my mind. I probably had but when you get to the end of your rope at times it's worth letting go and praying for the best.

My daughter choose to do the final page of the workbook. She completed it so well I marked the workbook as done and we moved on to the next. When we continued on I allowed her more freedom to set her own pace and she flew.

Convinced You Stink at Homeschooling?

What do you do when you think you stink at homeschooling? When your child didn't make the goals you had set for the year. You pulled them out of public school mid 4th grade but here we are at the end of the year and they aren't even able to do multiplication or read at grade level. Should you fail your child? Should you put your child back in school?

I highly doubt that you stink at homeschooling. You most likely just haven't found the right groove for your family yet. It can take time to get used to homeschooling and learning how to homeschool a child that doesn't match up to the books and curriculum out there can be daunting. Then the nosey nellies come poking their noses in letting you know what they think your child should know. How you must be failing to teach them right.

Sonya Haskins, a special needs homeschooling momma herself, hits the nail on the head. In her book *Homeschooling for the Rest of Us* she says, "Families who have a child with special needs aren't exempt from the pressure to be perfect. In many ways, these families probably feel more stress than other homeschoolers."[1]

We need to realize that people, even good intentioned ones, can be joy stealers. They will suck the joy out or your home and homeschooling adventure with surprising speed. Then you begin to feel homeschooling is drudgery. That will emotionally bleed over to our children even if we never speak a word to them about our feelings of inadequacy. Our kids will know and begin to grumble. Guard who you share your homeschooling details with, put up boundaries for others so that you can focus on your child rather than deal with the nosey nellies.

If you pulled your child out of school give it time. There will be an adjustment period for the entire family. Then it will take time to find the learning aptitude, use Subject Specific Learning techniques taught for the best fit. Realize that your child took years to come to this point of need. You will most likely not be able to fix their educational lag all in one year and that's okay. Set the pace of your homeschooling at your child's ability not their artificially set age/grade expectation. Remember that in a public school there are children that are not able to keep up with the average age/ grade standard as well. They are getting special accommodations and assistance. Being at home will make our life so much easier when it comes to adjusting to our child's immediate needs.

My Kid Is Failing! I Quit!

What about the touchy subject of grade advancement or retention. You are homeschooling so much of the paperwork struggle and burden is unnecessary. You are excelling past a simple passing grade to *mastery*, a true understanding of the needed concept. I encourage you to just keep going.

Through the years my family has dealt with a subject or several subjects that were not up to the age/grade expectation for that child. In order to prevent hurt feelings and continue learning, I cut the outside off the workbook set and used it with a "special homemade" cover. She needed to spend more time with the basic foundations of math before we moved on. It took time but then one summer there was a sudden leap forward in understanding. Homeschooling allowed me to give her time to learn and relearn and learn again if needed as many times as was necessary until she was ready to move on. Then when it clicked I could adjust our learning material closer to grade appropriate material quickly.

While my child's struggling did I hold her back technically grade wise? There was never an end to forward progress and continued learning. She was continuing to progress at the best speed she could.

Homeschooling When Learning Isn't Easy

In a public school system not all 6th graders will know how to multiply and divide. Some may never understand those concepts. Chris and I choose to keep moving forward as long as our child was putting in effort and the teacher we hired to help look over our material each year did not think we were missing important information. Progress however slow, is celebrated!

Speaking of celebrations, how many of you are considering graduation? I thought more about graduation in my first year of homeschooling than I did in my daughter's sophomore year. I kept thinking what if.. What if I don't know enough? What if I'm not good at this? What if I ruin my daughter's chance at graduating? I was wrong.

I was worrying, and that never gets you to a healthy place. I needed to calm down and focus on the place where we were. Yes, in late middle school we did need to think forward towards graduation and the possibility of college. I can assure you that early elementary is not when you need to be obsessing about high school. Let tomorrow worry about itself.

Some of our children are severely delayed or affected by their disability and will clearly not be going to an academic graduation or college. Do not see this as a sign of your homeschooling's failure, your failure, and of course not as your child's failure. Our goal as parents needs to be to produce godly productive adults to the best of their ability. Whatever that may be, we work towards it daily.

The majority of children and teens will go off to lead independent lives but ours will not. That is a lonely place. I have found over the years that autism was cute in the early years, but when my autistic toddler was melting down all over aisle three people didn't think it was nearly as cute. Then when that child was nine and laying on the floor at Target's, I got looks and told I was a miserable parent. Later, a 15 year old with loud tics, unusual conversation abilities, engaged one moment and then walking away mid-sentence. The older the child, teen and adult got the less cute and less tolerable the behaviors became. As parents of adult children with special needs we are a breed all on our own, sometimes literally on our own with no one nearby that understands.

Stressed and Locked in the Bathroom

You can continue to homeschool your child through the end of the public school's normal age range (usually 21 years old). You can get disability for your child if you go through the proper testing and your adult child gets awarded disability. You can also get guardianship, if necessary, when the time comes. Homeschooling should not be a problem with any of these life decisions. HSLDA has successfully pushed back at the social security disability department, courts, and school systems showing that homeschooling is completely adequate and loving way to raise a teen or young adult with severe issues.

When you choose your child's formal education is at an end, you can issue a parent signed Letter of Completion. Showing that your child had an education to the best of their ability. They tried and you are honoring them for that hard work.

No matter how you get from the beginning of your child's education to the end of the formal portion of homeschooling there is no right or wrong way to do it. In fact I often change up what I am doing and try to tweak things or find a new way to repeat old information that was not understood. Your wonderful family will have different hills and valleys then the person next to you at the support group. I want you to feel empowered to stay the course and have the courage to step out in faith when things are rough and you know you need to change.

Creating Your Own Support System

There are times and areas of the country that the homeschooling support structure is outstanding.

Jennifer had a great homeschooling community to connect with, "The homeschool community in our area is excellent, and I've been able to find terrific resources and instructors/mentors for him to work with."

Then there are times you have to take things into your own hands. Homeschooler support groups can be a wonderful help. I go to a "normal" support group. However there are special topics that need airing that can be difficult if you have never faced problems in your homeschooling journey. Potty training a 9 year old? A gifted child is reading the Hobbit at 6 and you want to share without others thinking you are bragging. It's time to build a special needs support group. I have found meeting once a month with other special needs parents to be refreshing and helpful in renewing my purpose to continue homeschooling through the ups and downs.

You can pull together a group of parents to have a support group yourself with these simple steps.

MAKING YOUR OWN SPECIAL NEEDS SUPPORT GROUP

Get the word out that you are starting a special needs home-schooling support group. **Talk to your state group and ask them to put it into their newsletter. Call the local co-ops and other support groups. Find local social media groups and ask to send out a message or email.** Get an idea of who would be interested and take down their contact info. You could also ask for suggestions on day, time, and location.

You need to pick a day, time, and location and set it in stone. The first Saturday of the month at 10 am in the First Baptist Church back school room. I like Saturday mornings because it can be difficult getting babysitters for special needs children and dad or grandparents would be home to care for them on Saturday. Knowing your child is being watched by dad helps relieve a ton of stress helping your support group be more relaxed and helpful.

That way if a parent misses one month they won't be wondering where to find the group. If you have irregular meeting times and places you will lose your membership over time and be left talking to a room by yourself.

Determine topics for the first couple of months. Find one that is wide based and leaves no one out, such as local paper work deadlines and how to fill them out properly. Then each month bring up a smaller topic that can really serve those coming, and encourage them to come! For example we had a curriculum provider come and show us the multitude of books and learning material that are out there. This was wonderful for us. We got to see and look through the books. It was great for the speaker because she made several sales that day, and long term networking with homeschooling parents.

There are ebbs and flows in attendance. Don't take it personally! Dedicate your time knowing you may be the only one there, but you will come again next month! Which reminds me, as you are building up the support group, there will be times you are there by yourself. It takes time to get people into a groove. It also takes time to build the relationships that help others come to trust and open up to a group. Be persistent and call a few days ahead of the meeting to gently remind your members. You could also send out an email reminder or contact them personally.

Also keep in mind that the time at the support group needs to be worth it. Have a speaker from the state organization come in and talk about the state law to be sure everyone is clear on it. Have a veteran mom come share her story of leading her children from birth through graduation. If you look around your area or the timing is right you might even get a professional speaker to come to your group and share. Chris and I are always open to speaking at groups along the way during speaking season when we are on the road. If we are already on the road to a convention in Dallas it's possible to speak to a group in Memphis, TN when normally that would be too far away from home. It becomes a win-win, and that provides worth and value to the whole group making your group stronger.

You should train someone to take your place if needed. We are a special needs group and health issues, accidents and emergencies happen. If you have planned ahead and put someone in that position they can pick up the meeting's agenda and lead the meeting.

Special needs homeschooling support groups may not be large groups but we are NEEDED groups. Our lives are generally lived one step (or more) outside normal. It is incredibly relaxing to sit and talk with other parents dealing with many of the same issues.

Relax Homeschooling Is Fun!

What a great job you are doing! You have taken on the full responsibility of parenting and teaching your child. You are to be commended for stepping up to do what is best for your child. Homeschooling isn't easy, and some days are better than others. Some subjects are easier to teach and easier for our children to learn. If you find that every day is a drudgery and a job to be done, you need to reevaluate what you are doing and how you are doing it. When enthusiasm has left the building, you need to find a way to refresh, restore, and renew your life. By fostering a love of learning and finding the balance between our wants and needs, we can create a healthier outlook on life, which naturally reduces stress and brings back the joy.

Patient persistent parenting will get you through the roughest periods. While the storms and valleys of life seem endless the vast majority of your time will be spent in a wonderful middle area of progress and bringing up your child to become a delightful adult. You can do it!

---

[1] Sonya Haskins, *Homeschooling for the Rest of Us* (Bethany House Publishers January 1, 2010)

Chapter 11: Excelling With a Medically Fragile Child

Did we choose to be different? No. It just snuck up on us quietly in the middle of a seizure, an asthma attack, at the bedside of one of my children in the hospital, or any one of a thousand other heart breaking moments that changed who we were. We didn't want this burden for our children but it's here.

Have you ever heard about the frog in the boiling water? The story goes if you put a frog into a pot of water and slowly turn up the water they won't notice. Eventually the water will be so hot it will be boiling. Yes, the frog is hurt but because the increase was so gradual they just kept adjusting to what was around them.

We have "frog in the boiling water" syndrome. Sure we might have gotten a shock as we were plopped in, whether that was a NICU baby or the diagnosis of a brain tumor when you were just thinking your child needed headache medicine but you learn very quickly that as mommy you need to put a good front up to encourage and support your child. Learn medical-speak fast so you know exactly what your child's doctor is talking about. And come to terms that your life just shifted sometimes radically but you learn to live with that tension fast because you have to. As mom or dad that's your job.

The boiling water soon becomes the norm and you put your head down and get through as best you and your family can. If someone else was plopped into the water next to us they would probably jump out right away realizing the situation was more serious than it appeared. Then they sit there panting, looking at you either with respect or horror given the intensity your life has become. Eventually we all get used to where we are and what we are dealing with no matter how extreme. I have five kids that all have a catastrophic disease. It is life shortening and heartbreaking. I have the same disease so not only am I dealing with the kids' differing abilities, medications, and specialist appoint ment but I have my own as well.

I can't just stop and take a break when I go to the hospital anymore because it is so often. Just because one of my littles needs yet another MRI doesn't mean we don't take homeschooling with us for the waiting room. It's not being mean or overachieving. It's life for my family and many others.

I think out of the box to make these, normal for us, moments learning fun. One appointment for ALL five kids with their neurologist is now an epic family story. The kids were learning anatomy of the brain. I found online these cute accurate printable brains. When our neurologist opened the exam room door she was met with a family of "Brainiacs". We all had on our paper brains, even dad joined the fun! By the end of the appointment the doctor had even posed in a brain to get a smile from the kids.

Make Medical Part of Your Life, or Medical Will Become Your Life!

Before I started scheduling time to make phone calls and set out needed medications I would find myself talking to a medical office in the middle of homeschooling. My kids would be drifting off long before the phone call was done. Then I would have to call everyone back to the table and go through moaning and groaning about that. It would suck up large chunks of time and enjoyment right out of home-schooling. The rhythm of our morning learning would be askew.

Now I have simple but cut and dried rules. All medical people I deal with either make their home visits or calls before 8:00am or after noon. That leaves all morning dedicated to learning new items, reading aloud, and working with each child. I carry my phone but I leave it in my pocket so I am not cruising the internet or answering emails. In short the only technology that is allowed, even for mom, in the mornings has to be homeschool related.

Dana loves the flexibility of homeschooling and told me," Home-schooling allows us to take days off when needed, such as days when he migraines are too much to bear."

You need to do things like this and take control of your medical life. Simple secret, if you don't take control of the medical it will take control of you. Your life could easily slip into a cycle of medication to medication. Appointment to appointment. Infusion to specialist to hospital stay and the joy of life fades in the sterile walls of the medical world. Fight back with fun out of the box thinking. Show your children that they are dealing with medical issue but they are in control of their outlook.

The Worst Clinic for Homeschoolers

Several years ago my daughter Rose was being prepped for a major surgery but her brother had a MRSA staph infection from a cut. In order to be cleared for the surgery Rose had to go to the infectious control medical department to be tested for staph herself. I had more than the usual amount of jitters at this appointment. My son had a serious infection. My daughter was going into have a Chiari decompression surgery (brain surgery). I had been told horror stories of how intrusive the infectious disease doctors could be into your life, even entering your home. I was emotionally spent and scared.

We went into the tiny appointment room and the doctor came in to start taking down the basic medical history. When he asked if she was in preschool.

I said, "No, we homeschool", and waited for the derogatory comment. It never came.

"Oh cool, my wife homeschools our two girls too!" He looked at Rose and said, "And I bet you love it!"

Rose turned on the charm then and talked his ear off for the rest of the appointment. Don't assume the worst! You just might find yourself talking to a homeschooled graduate or a homeschooler themselves!

Also the attitude towards homeschooling has changed and the medical community is trying to keep up.

The Medical Community

All of us will have to deal with the medical community at one point or another. Children have annual check-ups, they get sick, and let's face it, they get into everything.

My oldest had me on a first name basis with our local poison control operator. That was before I was educated on sensory seeking behaviors. I grimaced each time because I felt like a bad mom that my child had gotten into something possibly dangerous. She did get into some strange items but thankfully nothing that was "take her to the hospital" dangerous. With my second, third, fourth and fifth child I got much better at turning the house into Fort Knox.

I have felt a bit of fear when facing a doctor, therapist, or nurse who is questioning my child about schooling. The casual questions that doctors ask are often part of a social background the helps them understand the family better. For example if dad is employed then there is a much higher chance the child has food at home to eat. Also doctors are concerned that their patients get high quality care, therapy, and education. As we educate the medical profession the homeschooling intrusive questions will no longer be such a personal invasion. Instead medical professionals will accept the answer of homeschooling without hesitation.

Don't Forget the Medical Nosey Nellies

Just like your friends, the medical community will vary from homeschoolers themselves, to middle of the road as long as the kids are loved they don't care, to the extreme of anti-homeschoolers.

You have some ability to pick and choose making your life a bit easier. Ask around to your support groups, local co-ops ect. for homeschool friendly or at least tolerant doctors and therapists. Then do your best to educate if the opportunity arises, and generally show a normal family that happens to homeschool!

We had an unusual run in with a doctor ourselves. The doctor had seen our younger preschool aged child and was wonderful. We all laughed and had a pleasant appointment. Leaving with a treatment plan for our younger daughter.

About a year later a blood test for my oldest teenaged daughter meant we needed to see the same doctor. This time she came into the meeting with a second doctor. She quizzed my daughter only briefly on the symptoms and lab results. Then asked some social questions including what grade are you in. My children have never been given a grade like in a public school. I base their material off their ability and age.

My daughter politely replied she was 12 and in middle school. The doctor pressed her for a grade. My daughter laughed and said "I'm homeschooled. There is no need for a grade."

The previously pleasant happy doctor looked straight at the other doctor in the room and said, "Ohhh, they homeschool, tsk, tsk." Seriously, she tsked! The atmosphere changed immediately.

The temperature in that room dropped twenty degrees. My teenager felt it and I saw the raised eyebrow as a smirk pass from one doctor to the other. My daughter crossed her arms and legs and stopped talking. The doctor asked a few more questions but got little to no answer from my frustrated teen. Then the doctor said my teen was suffering from depression because of being deprived socially due to homeschooling. Her pain was not real and she did not have a "real" disease. Then pivoted to tell us to come back in six months since the labs did show a possible significant medical problem. I thought make your mind up doctor is there a problem and if so how is homeschooling impeding your ability to fix it?

We left and I hugged my daughter in the hall of the hospital. She had just met a doctor that ignored her very real pain because of a preconceived notion. I hurt so badly for my daughter. That was the last time we saw that particular specialist. I will not return for more possible belittlement of my teen or the possibility that her dislike of homeschooling could blossom into something that has social workers involved. Protect your children at all times from all angles.

If you get a doctor that is resistant to homeschooling understand you are hiring this doctor for their medical opinion. You can choose another doctor. You can tell them to restrain themselves to the medical issue only. If there is a major problem you can report this doctor to their hospital or superiors even the state medical board if necessary.

Keep in mind many people have not had exposure to homeschooling. The more doctors see homeschoolers are normal families and work just like the other families in their practice the more mainstream and acceptable we will be. One of our doctors when we first met him was disdainful of homeschooling. He is a great doctor so we decided to keep the homeschooling quiet and keep going to him. After several years of seeing him he asked if we were still homeschooling.

"Yes, we are." I told him, holding my breath to see what he would say. I was praying he would not get upset because the kids liked him, we liked him. He was helping the kids and if he got aggressive about this homeschooling we would have to leave.

"Great! Glad to hear it. I have thought about homeschooling my own daughter!" What a change! Well worth the slight changes we made to continue the doctor patient relationship.

Watchful Parenting Can Be Needed

Helicopter parenting is looked down upon but there are times watchful parenting must happen no matter what you call it. A child, teen or even an adult who cannot make proper health decisions, needs to be watched and guided carefully. If your teen is over 18 you might even need to become their guardian to be sure they make healthy life decisions.

Excelling With a Medically Fragile Child

Don't you love when you are talking to a person and they are waxing eloquent about how today's generation needs to just get up on its own two feet and parents are softies. On and on they go while I am turning a bright shade of red. You see, the good Lord blessed me with 4 children on the autism spectrum and all 5 have serious medical conditions. All 5 children are most likely going to need extra time staying in my home or they might be here for the rest of their lives, obviously not what this person is considering a help to society. Then suddenly I can see it dawning in their eyes. They remember who they are talking to. "Oh, but of course I didn't mean your children."

Hmmmm, not comforting. Mostly because I and my children face the sneers of people watching us, even calling security on us, when we use the handicap parking place. I see how when my child had a huge meltdown while we were leaving the library, several people were visibly mad at us and one person told me how to parent my child to "fix that problem", and on and on it goes. Thankfully these instances of discrimination are not every day. Some are just in passing and only rarely have we had a serious run in with a person who caused significant problems.

When you have a child or teen with a medical or mental health issue you can quickly became stretched thin and wonder what you are doing. Friends listen then suggest you send your child to school so you have "me" time. What they don't get is you don't really get me time. You get phone calls from the school to come in and calm your child, attend a meeting, pick up your child because they had an accident and the list goes on. Just now your life involves using lots of gas and the training and upbringing of your child is now in the hands of a team.

Let's be crystal clear here just because you chose to homeschool or adopt a child with special needs does not mean you aren't allowed to talk about the rough spots. You can groan like every other parent in a group over coffee then get back to work. It's human nature to want support from your friends and family not guilt or admonishments that I brought this on myself. My children are already getting all of my energy, if you my dear friend or family member choose to make my life stressful I will need to put up a boundary between us to lower the stress in my life. You need to create a healthy support group around your family that is full of people that are helpful, full of joy, and understanding!

Raising a child with medical issues is physically and emotionally exhausting. You have to be on your toes ready to jump into action 24/7. Medications and nebulizers run all day and night. Many children with medical challenges also often have problems with sleeping. That means you don't sleep if they are little or have limited ability to care for themselves. When these issues go on day after day, week after week, even year after year you enter a level of survival mode that has be likened to combat veterans.

I like that homeschooling lets us change up the normal "sun up go to school" paradigm. If our teens are night owls and work best past 10pm then I am willing to work with that up to a point. If my child has to sleep after an infusion of IVIG then they do. When they wake up we will work with what they are able to and later in the week we can add a bit more here and there to catch up.

Many families enjoy the daily schedule adjustments, Dana shared, "I do not wake them (the kids) because allowing them to sleep as much as their body needs is important to aiding in control of their disorder." Talking about her children's epilepsy.

There are some options like family, friends, and respite care. Friends and family who are willing to step in and give you a few hours of un-interrupted sleep are a Godsend. I know, I was there! Respite care from outside sources is rare and hard to come by. It also costs a pretty penny if are having to pay for it straight out of your pocket. There are also home health care, palliative care and hospice assistance that can allow you time to go to the store or rest.

When the Medical Problem Could Be Terminal

When you are dealing with a child that has a terminal disease your world has shifted. It will never be the same again. You have so much to deal with emotionally that the urge to go back to bed and pull the covers over your head and cry is strong.

Excelling With a Medically Fragile Child

People in general understand what a prognosis of cancer with a couple of months to live means. People are much less able to understand that a terminal illness like cystic fibrosis or the condition my children and I have, mitochondrial disease, means that we don't know when we may die. It could be today with a stroke. It could be a year from now with an infection that our bodies can't fight.

If your child is dying, then you have tons of medical appointments. Usually schools are good about working with you on a shorter term basis but again as the weeks turn to months and longer, their patience may wear thin. Truancy court will not make your life easier. I have a friend from high school whose child has a known chronic illness that requires infusions and repeated stays in the hospital. She has an IEP and open communication with the school and her child's teacher. The problem is, at the administrative level, the paperwork shows her as repeatedly truant. This family has had to go to court several times. Homeschooling allows you to deal with these repeated medical needs without the intrusion of layers of bureaucracy.

As illness impacts your child's abilities you can keep adjusting to what works the best. I do recommend you keep working. There is no line in the sand. Keeping a mind active is most of what learning should be. Delight in the journey rather than the end result of a piece of paper.

After the diagnosis of mitochondrial disease for all five children it took time the great equalizer for the numbness to begin to wear off. We quietly told some of our close family what was happening there were many questions, tears, and an understanding of what we were facing that took many months and conversations. Eventually as the truth of our situation sank into our family and friends the question was raised, "Are you going to continue homeschooling?"

Why would you homeschool through such a terribly difficult time? I want to spend every second with my family that I possibly can. I want to be able to show them every sunrise, the ocean, the plains of Kansas. I don't want my children to be hemmed in by four walls and a fence for most of the year, most of the day, for the majority or possibly all their life. We are building a treasury of memories that will stay with us always.

Homeschooling When Learning Isn't Easy

We enjoy homeschooling and are deeply committed to continuing. I can't say that everyone understood our reasoning, or even agreed with homeschooling. Considering our children's medical condition and four of them have autism so we needed to be acutely aware of their emotional fragility. When the kids were young we would often have to walk a very fine line of going to the big family get together or not. Should we go and face possible spread of a cold or disease from other young cousin that could devastate our children's health? Then there were some family members that were part of the public school system that delighted in pelting me or the kids with questions.

Chris and I created a plan for times like these. If we decided to go to the get together. Double check all cousins for signs of illness, like red fever cheeks. Let the kids have a great time as long as they were able. Take along our gluten free food so there would be no fuss about food. As for the adults, Chris would help me if I was cornered. I would do the same for him. If the questioning or attitude got out of hand we would leave.

We want the children to have all the best we can give them. From family get togethers to the best education to a life that is filled with love and as best we can easing the burden of their disease. There is a question that comes up often in the quest to give our kids the very best, "Am I keeping them from something special by keeping them from public school?" What changed from yesterday?

Life is not perfect. It isn't today and it won't be when my kids grow up. Showing the kids now that they can keep going through the hard times and never give up is worth the hard work.

My homeschooling life is unique. I teach my kids from my hospital bed. There is a table placed at the end of the bed where the kids can pull their wheelchairs up to or sit and work. We schedule our life around multiple doctor appointments and the occasional hospital visit. We are not your average family. Yet we are successfully and joyfully homeschooling. I know you too can have a wonderful homeschooling experience!

Homeschool Creates a Life of Unique Opportunities

We are blessed. The joy of homeschooling has provided a unique and very flexible lifestyle. We are able to travel often and share each and every day together.

Homeschooling allows the flexibility to keep going. There are times when we homeschool sick and in the hospital. It helps to take your mind off what is happening and the hospital is possibly one of the most boring places in the whole world.

It has allowed us to hold class on the beach, feeling the wind brush your cheeks for the first time. One year into hospice I got to see the delight in my youngest child's eyes as she saw the ocean for the first time. That moment, in the middle of the week as the harvest moon rose across the water, has been etched into my daughter's and my hearts. We were able to truly appreciate the moment together.

I am a mommy. I am hardwired to fix my children's problems. Prepare for them for a long healthy life and someday launch them off into adulthood. I worry because there is a fog in my family's future. The boo boos cannot be kissed away. I will be honest with you, there is a corner of my mind that thinks because I can't fix my children and assure them a long lovely life I have failed them. Then I realize that it is not up to me to designate how long any of us are here on earth. I trust God and trust his plan.

Children shouldn't die. We have found that many people's gut reaction is to pull away from even thinking about it. We lost many friends when the diagnosis of mitochondrial disease was even suggested. The truth is children all around the world struggle with progressive diseases, horrible accidents, and some die at an early age. Their lives were not lost because of their brevity. The Lord didn't ignore your pleas for healing. There are some things that cannot be healed here on earth, so they will be healed in Heaven.

I will not look away from the face of a child with cancer and dying because it crosses over my comfort level. I will embrace them, and their parents. I will do the very best I can to give that child or family a moment of peace, acceptance, and I pray hope.

Allowing Grief to Start the Healing Process

I cannot fully express to you the pain I feel for you. After being told that the genetic disease we deal with as a family is life shortening I was stunned. I can truly say I was numb to anything but the doing of life. My emotions short circuited, there was too much to process. I can only imagine what you are feeling by the prognosis of my children's disease and how it plays out in my head. I offer you my deepest prayers and sympathy.

How much should you tell your child? Many children already know there is something wrong. Whether you are in a situation where there is an acute injury like a car crash, chronic illness, or a possibly terminal issue like cancer. Hiding the problem and tip toeing around the illness may encourage your child to bottle up their feelings. We have to at this time of illness be as open as our child is able to handle including using assistance from palliative care or hospice care teams to work through the emotional pitfalls.

The older your child the more they notice but may not be able to apply adult logic to. You must keep talking about what is happening. When questions come I have always found it best to answer them honestly and briefly. Allowing your child or teen to work through their own cycle of grief at the change in their life. They are mourning a life they had planned out too whether it is because of the realization that they may never marry, or dad may not live to see them marry, or that he will but he will be in a wheelchair.

The intensity of caring for a dying child or parent has passed. In its wake the silence can be deafening. Do not push yourself or your child to resume a "normal" life. Things have changed, like a Fabergé egg that has been broken it cannot be put back together perfectly ever again.

That does not mean you won't find a new normal. You will. Your family will grieve. The rawness will pass. Homeschooling at times like these is secondary to your emotional healing.

Feel free to set aside the books, field trips and other obligations. Welcome the meals from your friends and take strength from their hugs. Show your children your grief. Share with them their feelings. Together you will make it!

Chapter 12: Making It Work When Mom's Sick

"**Y**ou have stage 4 cancer," the doctor told Hal Young of Raising Real Men. He had a fifty-fifty chance of making it through the year. If that had been the only thing going on in their life it would have been devastating but the previous year had been a buildup of medical nightmare after medical nightmare. A daughter born with a heart defect that was life threatening. A son that needed an extensive foot surgery and follow up. Again and again they were smacked down with medical problems and the extreme financial issues that come with medical care. However this family of ten kept homeschooling and did so with a joyful spirit.

Homeschooling Through the Storms of Life

Hal and his wife Melanie are strong believers in the Lord and in homeschooling. They are blessed with a large wonderful family of six boys and two girls. They believe so deeply that homeschooling is the best educational option out there they have poured years of their lives and time into helping others homeschool. Whether through working with their state or speaking on a national level they continue to be strong proponents of homeschooling. Even in the midst of these medical storms they continued to care for the homeschooling community.

The diagnosis threw them for a loop. A heart attack, maybe. Others in the family had experienced early heart problems so it was "on their radar" but cancer was not on their list of things to be concerned about. Despite all the things they had going on and all the treatments they were facing in the near future, homeschooling kept going. They knew they would need to adjust their home life but they also knew that as a team with the Lord's help and strength they would make it.

They trusted God's plan and outcome no matter what. I know them from speaking at conferences. Our families met just after Hal had his last chemotherapy. You wouldn't have known unless you noticed that he went to the hotel room to rest and protect his immune compromised body. This family shined in their darkest hour.

Later Hal had to go through testing to see if the doctors had stalled the cancer or if it was progressing. The doctor was stunned by the test results. Hal and Melanie called their children awaiting the news at home and shouted over the phone the great news that Hal was, "CANCER FREE"!

One teenaged son ran to the front yard and with tears of joy he praised the Lord and thanked him for his father's healing! This family pulled together and worked through the years of rough times. Hal and Melanie didn't hide the problems they were facing from the children but they were careful to be age appropriate for each child's ability and understanding of what was happening.

Melanie shared with me, "It would have been really scary to the little ones to overhear what was happening from someone else rather than being told by mom and dad."

Telling their children what was happening, showing them how to struggle and survive through the storms in life turned out to be a wonderful unscheduled homeschooling lesson that will help their children throughout their lives. By sharing the depths of their struggle, the family was also able to truly see the heights of the mountain tops and beauty of that one little sentence, "Cancer free!"

Too Sick to Homeschool

Homeschooling is truly a family activity. If mom or dad has a health problem, it impacts the whole family, including homeschooling. How you deal with health problems will depend on what you're dealing with. Is this an acute issue that will go away within a couple of months or a chronic issue that you need to learn to live with? Balancing your health and running the family can, at times, be challenging but always worth it! We will be teaching our children empathy, caring, healthy living, and emotional fortitude under difficult times. All these lessons will make for a stronger more capable adult someday.

I often hear parents concerned that their illness might bring down their child. They could make their child miss out on important events and opportunities that children with healthy parents get to enjoy. Maybe you're afraid that caring for a chronically ill parent will end up sucking the joy out of their childhood I have seen parents who are given a diagnosis, such as cancer or lupus, and they send their children back to public school without even trying to make it work.

I understand the urge to protect your child from the harsh realities that life sometimes dishes out. Let me urge you not to give up on homeschooling. I believe that even during the darkest time homeschooling will shine and be a benefit to your family. By sharing the hard times with our children we are imparting a gift of perseverance that cannot be taught from any book. Children and teens learn to look beyond themselves when they are helping their father or mother. By showing strength in the face of adversity we are raising stronger more capable children.

I am not going to tell you whether or not you are too sick to homeschool. I want you to know that there are families that are quietly homeschooling through some of the worst storms life has to offer. They are doing so successfully. There are times that the academics have to be put aside to deal with the emotional and logistical life issues that are occurring. Families are finding ways to make homeschooling happen or they are turning to out of the box alternatives such as a semester in private school while mom gets chemotherapy with the hopes of returning to homeschooling later. There will be no shaming here! What works for your family is what is best for your family and I support you in your decision. Let's just be sure we have prayed this through and thought about it from different angles. Remember take and use only that which enriches and helps your family. Leave the rest including the guilt behind. We are moving forward!

Logistics We Need to Consider

The worst words I can hear from my husband in the morning, "I didn't sleep. I'm flaring." That means my poor husband is exhausted and in pain. A type of pain that even his medication only somewhat moderates. That day will not be the day to ask him to start my kitchen remodeling project, take the kids on a field trip or do much more than nap!

As homeschoolers we can take a day off like that but we can't do that every day or even for a series of days. For those of us that are naturally schedule challenged, a single day off can linger into two days and then three because daddy is still flaring and needs to nap. I get it, but we have to work out a way to keep homeschooling going even when our bodies are fighting us.

Our friends and family will give us a pass and say "Oh, take the day off. You are hurting and you deserve it," that's nice but not practical over the long term. If I took every day off that I hurt and was nauseous or needed help to get to the table to homeschool we would fall too far behind. That with the autism would mean we would be off schedule and my house would soon devolve into nothing but a tech time marathon or agitated children that didn't feel right because the schedule was being ignored.

Finding the place of balance where you give yourself grace and a day off and keeping on going is up to you. I tend to push through early in the week because I never know if later in the week will be worse. I also tend to push through early in our 6-8 week cycle for the same reason. I never know when I will be in the hospital. I will also pull something together if we take more than three days off. The only exception is if the kids are sick too and we have something like the flu. Then everyone gets to snuggle up with their blanket, a book, and the dog (after a skirmish over who gets the dog).

Have a "sick schedule" and a "normal schedule". For each of us that is going to be different because normal to you might mean swollen joints that don't move in the morning due to lupus or you might have multiple medications you need to balance or you might aim your homechooling for a time of year when you function the best and do have a more typical homeschooling lifestyle. The sick days are the ones that you need your children to be more independent. Focus on the subjects that are hard to catch up with like math, reading, or therapy sessions. There is quite a calming effect to having stability in the home and schedule.

Have you considered the grass is greener in the public school system? Think of how hard it would be to get your child out the door to school every day and then pick them up. If your child has a special need you will need to address that as well through school visits and IEP meetings. Then you will need to deal with transitions home, homework, some schools have mandatory volunteer hours, etc. There is also the idea however false it is that your child begins to think you want time away from them. Or they were making you sick so sending them to school will make you better. We need to look at this situation from many angles and in the end while it may require outside help such as grandparents or other homeschooling parents, possibly even a mommy's helper (which could be a responsible high school or college student) I really think homeschooling is a wonderful solution to our unique family's needs.

Helping Your Home Run Smoothly

When you are the special need in the family stress and guilt tends to creep into your heart. You allow others to pick at you with their words like the Nosey Nellie or Cathy with a Cure person in your life that know just how to fix you and if you say no then you obviously enjoy being sick. Let's clear that up now. No one I know likes feeling sick, tired, in need of medications especially when they have so much to live for. Those loving faces that you wake up for each day are ready to learn from you and help you in any way they can!

The first step to helping de-stress is to ignore and put up boundaries in your life removing those that are harmful to you or your children emotionally. Surround yourself with healthy wonderful people. Friends and family that are ready to assist, pray, and be a shoulder to lean on when you need it. Have these wonderful people on call as back up just in case you get so sick you need to go to the doctor or hospital. That way you know your children will be safe. You have a safety net in place.

Let's deal with everyday life. Those pesky kids just want to eat three solid meals a day and usually a couple of snacks. We are a gluten free household so meals always take a bit of forethought. Now that I am sick and Chris is dealing with fibromyalgia I need to be a couple steps ahead of the meals at all times. I have started doing all my shopping for the seven people in my home only once a month. We bring home the food and prepare it that night. The next couple of days I will turn it all into meals for the coming month. Then I know that we have healthy good meals for the whole month that will be easy to defrost or throw in the slow cooker. It a tremendous amount of pressure off my day.

Another way to help our homeschooling continue while I am going through a rough patch is Saturday school with daddy. It was a time when daddy would teach the new concepts of math or do science experiments with the kids when I was too sick to do them myself. Sometimes even going out to do field trips that I did not have the energy or ability to take them on during the week. Working together insured that the children's education never suffered and I never pushed myself beyond a healthy level of activity.

Guilt is the ultimate stressor in anyone's life. You have to let the guilt go. Block out those trying to guilt you from the outside and shut down that inner nagging voice. You can do that by reminding yourself of the reason you are homeschooling, remember we wrote that on the inside of our lesson planner. Go back to it and reread often if necessary, I do. Another way to defeat guilt is to step back and see all the wonderful work your child has done. If you have been keeping a portfolio pull it out and look over all the great things your child has learned this year. Think of all the intangible things like learning to say thank you or please or having your young son open the door for someone. We are aiming for the big picture friends. We are guiding our children to become godly productive adults to the best of their ability and our special need as a parent will be used as a tool to help them if we ask the Lord in prayer.

Pregnancies Don't Always Run Smooth

Dealing with a rough pregnancy and homeschooling is not easy. If you are prone to nausea tending to your kids meals and snacks just make you feel worse. Then the pressure and stress we moms tend to put on ourselves to get through x amount of lessons before the baby comes doesn't help. If you are on bedrest trying to maintain some form of sanity and a clean home can be next to impossible especially if you don't have anyone outside your home to come in and help. Rough pregnancies can be difficult while homeschooling but they are not impossible.

Let's talk real life, what if you're on bed rest right now? I have a whopping big BTDT (Been There Done That) t-shirt for modified bedrest. I was blessed with a wonderful almost perfect pregnancy the first time then all seven pregnancies after that had some sort of medical issue. My final full term pregnancy was the worst. I was on bed rest eleven weeks!

At the time I had four little ones, three with autism and all four were taking some of therapy. Daddy had just taken a job that was three hours away and that meant he had to leave the house on Sunday night and not come home until Friday! All while on bedrest. I was stretched THIN.

We got through this time safely and I have a lovely eight year old to show for the hard work. Don't let anyone tell you that laying there on your left side all day is not hard work. It is! Made worse when you have littles that you are sure need you to get up and clean up the socks on the floor. I had to tune that all out and focus on only the very basics of homemaking. I had to ask for help. I needed to pull together the family and we all had to work towards the goal of letting mommy lay on the couch to keep baby sister healthy.

First, daddy is a rock star! He would do all the laundry during the weekend. He would make all the meals for the week. Any shopping that needed to be done he would load the whole crew up and take them with him to the store. He even got them all cleaned up dressed and pressed to go to church Sunday morning so they got to see their friends and keep the routines of church that they were used to.

We were blessed that time for the bedrest to work. The next time it did not. Sadly my final pregnancy ended in a miscarriage. It was emotionally very difficult, more so than my other stillbirth and miscarriage because I knew I would never have another child. I choose to keep homeschooling our normal schedule as closely as possible. Not because I wanted to act like losing Abigail never happened but because I needed a strong structure to my life to deal with the hormonal blues and the emotional low due to her loss.

Please if you have a miscarriage allow yourself time to heal physically and emotionally. You will have all those hormones in your system for months. Acknowledge that you just gave birth whether that little one was five weeks or thirty-seven weeks. You and your family need to grieve the loss.

It's okay to cry. It's okay to change your routine for something fresh and different. It's not healthy to be so lost in tears that you can't stop: to feel so low that you begin imagining dark things like taking your life. If you feel this way call your doctor immediately.

I am not a doctor or counselor. I can tell you that when I lost my daughter to a devastating birth defect I lost my way. I became very depressed. My husband and midwife noticed and helped me. I did take medications for a time to get things under control and then I could stop. I am thankful that there are medications that will help when you get that low. Don't be afraid to ask for help.

My heart goes out to you. I am sorry you have this pain to carry. You are not alone. The storm you are walking through will lighten. You won't ever forget or leave behind your precious child. Instead you will move forward with your life and carry that precious child in your heart until the day you meet them face to face in Heaven.

Mom or Dad Have a Short Time to Live

As a parent there are certain implied responsibilities such as changing diapers, losing sleep, teaching your child how to ride a bike, helping a teen with their driver's test, and most of all parenting your child to adulthood. Being a grandparent someday. Growing old with your husband or wife. When your life is counted in seasons rather than years you can feel like your life has just been wrenched from your grasp and limited. There are so many questions to ask. Should you stop homeschooling? Would it be better on yourself or your child to send them to school? How will watching me die affect my child? Would it be easier on my child if they were in school, away from me and my illness for hours a day?

I am living out that quandary. I am dying. The same genetic disease that my children have I gave to them. Several years ago I had a stroke that was near my brain stem and has started a downward decent in my health. I am now on hospice working through each day at a time. Dealing with each medical issue at a time. While my children are also dealing with the disease. We decided, like the Young's, to continue to homeschool.

Homeschooling is not just because we are sick. We homeschool because Chris and I feel that the Lord has placed this precious responsibility of our children into our care and tending. The basis of why we homeschool has not changed because of my health. This goes back to why are you homeschooling? That written reason and goals for our homeschooling life we talked about earlier that you will refer to during the storms of life and will be reaffirmed.

I listen to my mommy friends and hear about all the great co-ops, and field trips. I want to turn back to a time when I could take my kids on those same trips. Now I cannot drive because of my stroke and seizures so no quick trips to the zoo. Not even a quick run to the grocery store. I have to plan like a military action to get to the store for our once a month shopping trip. I am not in the least upset at my friend's ability to drive and do those spur of the moment field trips. . It just highlights the fact that our situation has changed.

Homeschooling When Learning Isn't Easy

Those dealing with chronic illnesses will understand the flares of fatigue and illness that suck the life out of you with no notice. I used to be the mom that had a full yummy meal on the table after a day of homeschooling, canning, running to a friend's house for the kids to play. Now I am so weak that there are days I lead our homeschooling from my hospital bed. We have our meals planned out far in advance and they tend to be crockpot meals or simple oven baked meals. It hangs heavy on my heart when I have to rely on cold cereal and leftovers for dinner because I'm too tired to make anything else. Yes, I know that leftovers won't hurt my kids. I guess I see it as an outward sign of my physical weakness.

I want to be that active energetic mom I was a few short years ago. That time has passed. I won't ever be that person again. I have needed to come to peace with that. I have needed to understand that my illness takes up time from my day. Time to dole out medications, hook up IVs, TPN (Total Parental Nutrition), talk with nurses, insurance, and schedule more appointments. I have started scheduling time into my day so I wasn't "stealing" time from other things in my life like my kids and homeschooling.

I am not the mom I wanted to be. Not the outgoing, healthy, well balanced, busy mom I always imagined. I am facing things that I shouldn't have to deal with until I am seventy but here I am on hospice and learning a new way of life. One that is clearer and more focused than ever on what is worthwhile and meaningful in my life. God and my family.

I never thought about being a mom in constant pain. A mom that fights seizures. That can't even eat food anymore. I ache for the dream of a life I desperately *wanted* to give my kids. I never once imagined being the one to die and leave my husband widowed raising our precious children alone. It's my responsibility to be here helping. But no matter how hard I try my body is not able. I am fighting the waves of the tide as it slowly comes in. I ache for a life that is long enough to see my children graduated. There are times like today that I find I have nowhere else to run. I have to face the reality that my future and my present are not what I dreamed, or planned. I will continue to need medical intervention to live. I will need medications to live. And I will need to learn a new way to live that life including parenting my children.

There are things I have to do for when the time comes that my chapter here on earth is over. I need to be sure that I have, to the best of my ability, readied my husband, children and our life (including homeschooling) to handle my passing intact. I need to prepare now and then set the preparations aside and live a wonderful life for as long as I am blessed with it.

Frankly, this is the part of the book that I never wanted to be able to write. I don't want to plan for a future without me here as mommy or without my beloved husband as support. Life has shown me that we MUST as good stewards of our home make plans for the best possible outcome as well as the worst. Once made you can set those plans aside and live life to its fullest knowing you have done a fine job covering a just in case scenario.

As the main homeschooling teacher in my home there are things that I have done to deal with any legal issues up front. I have gotten a will. I have also started legacy letters to those that I love explaining my decisions and directions upon my passing. I have given my husband full medical power of attorney so my soul mate is the one making decisions if I cannot. I keep records in an easy to find place of all the years of homeschooling, and I have talked my husband through it all. I went over exactly what the state requires of us each year and when. As for the material I have lesson plans and goals written out. I also have chosen to go with a more text oriented material (as per my husband's request) so the lessons are easier for him to pick up and continue.

While my natural relaxed nature towards homeschooling works great for many it was not a good common sense choice with me as sick as I am. This was highlighted when I had a particularly nasty illness called sepsis. I spent several weeks in the hospital. My husband had to leave his job and come home. My previous relaxed structure of homeschooling left him with five children with special needs that were all at different places in unit studies, read aloud books, flash card work, file folder games, high school German and frankly it was a mess, or so I was

Homeschooling When Learning Isn't Easy

told. We realized when I came home in order to keep the continuity of learning we had to have a more structured homeschooling lesson plan.

We talked about what he needed to be able to homeschool the kids if ever that should happen again. Chris told me that he needed a laid out written idea of where we were and what he needed to teach. I decided to use a planner that had each child's path clearly laid out. I chose to use more textbook/workbook oriented material for the structure of our homeschooling. Then I filled in the blanks with unit studies, group book studies, and other enriching materials. The final piece to creating our groove was to finalize a routine to post on the wall so everyone could see and follow.

If you ever find yourself in a situation where you need another person to step in and help out, keep a folder full of fun ideas for the family to follow. If it's an acute short term thing having an extended holiday filled with fun, service, and projects might be a perfect fit. Don't be afraid to say I am too sick to teach right now. In order to be a good parent and hopefully a healing parent you must get rest, good nutrition, and lower stress. Take care of yourself and teach your child to be mindful of their own health. These are the intangible but highly useful lessons that everyone needs to learn.

When I am gone I trust in the Lord to watch over my children and husband. I trust in my husband to take up the mantle of homeschooling dad and sole caregiver to our children. I don't think it will be easy but I know he can do it. That doesn't mean I want to go anywhere!

Always be hopeful, doctors can be wrong! Miracles do happen!

Chapter 13: Your Delightfully Different Path

"**Y**ou're homeschooling how many kids?" The woman gasped as she took in all five of my children in their unique sensory garb and medical mobility galore.

We were sitting in a specialist's waiting room for a visit with ALL 5 kids. She and I had been chatting quietly while our children played until I mentioned homeschooling.

"You have five kids with mitochondrial disease and four have autism." She began leaning back in her seat away from me.

We weren't just the family with an illness, we were weird and it was written across her face that she couldn't get away from us fast enough.

I have even heard much worse renditions on the same theme, up to the point of strangers questioning why I would have a child with a disability willingly? My answer is okay so which one of these smiling kiddos do you want me to send back? Or which of their three angel sister/brothers should I have not had?

Special needs brings out the extremes in people particularly if the special need is visible. However I would like to focus on the more common reaction we get as a family. Smiles, joy, wonderful compliments, doors held open, prayer support from complete strangers and so much more.

Recently we went as a family to a business conference. All seven of us in a van packed full for eight hours of travel. We have to bring two power wheelchairs, a walker, all our gluten free food, medications (including oxygen tanks), extra sensory items and the list that is literally two pages single spaced long goes on. That is what we need to go on the road and maintain our schedule as best as we can for the children's sake and our health needs.

Homeschooling When Learning Isn't Easy

After that huge trip we piled out into the parking lot of the unsuspecting hotel. One child had her Halloween monkey costume on (sensory issue). One child was screaming for no reason I could see or ever found I just had to let her go on screaming while I hugged her for several minutes. Another child could hear the beach and being my eloper (a child that has little danger sense of wandering away), off she went. Daddy has eyes in the back of his head so he stopped her and we began the "Grand Distraction". That means we distract and focus the kids on specific tasks until we can get them all into the hotel room.

Hotel rooms are actually easy to deal with since they are a clean slate and we set up our home away from home in under an hour. For seven people, we should get an award for that!

Then in the setting sun with a full moon that night we all went down to the beach. The kids were beachcombing and for my youngest it was her first experience with the ocean. I usually use a power wheelchair to get around but it was not possible to even get to the dune line in my chair. I used my walker and family to help me get to the beach. I had a powerful desire to feel the ocean between my toes one last time and the added bonus of being my birthday. The whole family pitched in and helped to carry, drag and encouraged me all the way down to the wave line.

While I am not a big fan of the name, I ticked off another thing on my bucket list. My family was there to enjoy it with me and that was phenomenal. Our family was on a business trip, family vacation, and one big field trip that we would not have been able to go on if the kids were bound by the public school calendar.

This trip and the night time walk on the sand was so much more to me as mom and wife. I am extremely sick and my muscles are failing. This will most likely be the last time I can feel the ocean and the sand. Given that my hubby and I met in Navy boot camp and I lived in Puerto Rico for a time the importance of sharing this moment with my children was magnified tremendously. Homeschooling gave us the time and flexibility to have this family trip.

Your Delightfully Different Path

Just so you know this trip, while having huge emotional importance, was a vital portion of the fall semester for my children's homeschooling. You can have a vacation and homeschool all while having a wonderful time. How in depth can you take a simple getaway like this beach trip? Cute for the elementary kids but what about my high schoolers you might be thinking? I had a senior that year and she was able to come home and research the many things they found on the beach. We found out while we were there, that the whelks were hatching. My senior found science videos and oceanography learning material online and through our Apologia science curriculum to bring the experience to a well-rounded higher level learning experience.

Homeschooling Is Possible!

Homeschooling is legal in all 50 states, including for those with special needs. You can find a wide variety of support to help you along the way. From local groups, state groups, to large conventions and online groups that are ready to help out. We discussed how you can create your own special needs support group. I run a large social media and blog membership groups for special needs homeschooling. Using online support and the vast pool of experienced parents out there is very helpful.

You can find curriculum, textbooks, workbooks, co-ops and specialized tutoring programs. It is all very possible today. The doors have been flung open and the homeschooling world is being given the top tier of educational material! You can embrace multiple platforms and methods of learning. I use online programs, textbooks, workbooks, unit studies, and lap books. Don't forget play and good old construction paper and flashcards. Learning happens where you allow an imagination to run free and you provide an enriched loving home.

Homeschooling Is a Responsible Choice!

You can find all the learning material fitted directly to your child's needs using Subject Specific Learning techniques. Remember to match your child's weakest area to their strongest learning mode.

Then find the material that fits that subject. Next, do the opposite with their strongest subject. You will be helping your child become a well-balanced learner able to eliminate, remediate, or accommodate their special needs.

Homeschooling any child, especially a child with special needs, is not a choice you just bumbled into with no thought. You know that by choosing to homeschool whether you felt forced to make that decision because of a safety situation, IEP failure or you started homeschooling and things weren't happening as expected it is now our responsibility. It can be a weighty burden but one that is worth the hard work and effort. It gets easier to bear the longer you homeschool. Surround yourself with those who will support your family and parental decisions.

Am I asking you to reinvent education just to create homeschooling for your family? No, I am not. What I am cautioning against is using someone else's standards, material, or homeschooling program that makes your family into theirs. Look around, read books, go to conventions, read blogs and magazines to get ideas. I have started consultations and other means like e-courses to help you find your unique learning path. Finding others that you can pick and choose the very best for your child is exactly what will help you develop into a high functioning and happy homeschooling family.

We Are a Vibrant Community!

I had to take a breather. I pulled my wheelchair over to the side of the walkway. I was at a convention center overflowing with people. Where I sat I could see escalators packed with people trying to get to the next set of workshops. Groups of teens walking in and out of classrooms, texting as fast as they could. Families of every size and composition were walking or running through the halls depending on how fast the toddler of the group was going. The entire convention center was filled.

You would never have known they were homeschoolers. This group of people would have looked just as comfortable if placed in Disney and or some other family event. Homeschoolers don't fall into any set mold. We are delightfully different!

Homeschooling is a unique form of education that will help you meet the needs of each of your children. It's not a matter of follow the leader or buy the priciest product to produce the best scholarship. Homeschooling is not at its best helping your family achieve their goals until it is tailored to you. It should be molded to meet your needs not you changing to meet the needs of a textbook. For our special learners, this is even more imperative. We keep in mind our rate of skill development, maturity, and learning style versus the learning product we are trying to use.

Our children no matter their strengths or weaknesses will thrive with homeschooling. You will have the opportunity to knit together a family that is closer emotionally, spiritually and intellectually than with any other educational choice. Learning together along the way in an enriched and nourishing lifestyle.

Dana found homeschooling to be a beautiful journey with her children. She shared, "I wish I had known that it would be this easy, this much fun, this amazing of an experience. I wish I had known that it would help to build a relationship with my children that we would never have had if we had chosen not to homeschool. I also wish I had realized sooner that I have 365 days to cover materials and that means I don't have to teach every subject every day."

Your child is not the sum of their disabilities. No, we are blessed by their strengths and uniqueness!

Homeschooling Is Successful!

Success is a moving measurement in the educational system these days. Choose a higher option for your child. Mastery of skills. Take each skill one at a time and learn them to mastery. Your child will excel so much better in later years if they have mastered the basics. Even if they take longer to learn the basics, when it clicks I have seen firsthand how successful it can be. How a teen with a desire to learn and purpose to their life simply flew ahead!

Can homeschooling a special needs child really help? YES! You can get learning material that you pick just for your child's strengths and weaknesses crafting a lesson plan with subject specific learning techniques. You can have a more intense therapy schedule if necessary. If your child needs multiple doctor appointments instead of missing class and losing ground you take the material with you. Your child will be less stressed and anxious at home. They will be exposed to less viruses. You can provide a one to one environment that is necessary for many children to learn.

Homeschooling your special needs child can be a wonderful family enriching opportunity! Many kids need quantity time not short intense quality, particularly if they have developmental delays or have slower processing abilities. The more you and their siblings are there, the better the relationship will be. Yes, kids grump at each other but see this as a way to teach conflict resolution! Use your home and the daily ups and downs to show your child life skills they will need now and as an adult on their own.

My husband Chris and I have realized over the years that the Lord has brought us to a ministry to help special needs families. We are here to assist you in your calling to homeschooling. Some of you are at the end of your rope and have no other option but to homeschool. We are here to help you find joy again and find your foundation. How to create a homeschooling lifestyle that is enriched fulfilling your child's unique needs allowing them to blossom. We are here to help you move from a place of frustration and being unsure of your ability to homeschool, to a more confident parent ready to tackle homeschooling!

It's time to bring peace to your home, to stop the battle with behavioral, medical and heart issues and become a vibrant loving home. Finding ways to reinforce the family and sibling bonds like family meals. We are working towards creating godly productive adults to the best of their ability. We are setting high standards that are matched to our

hild's abilities and going for the big dream that God has envisioned
or them. We are loving parents, you bet we can dream big!

Our job as parents is be the protector of the big dream. We hold
t and help it to flourish, guiding our children towards a future that is
outstanding and made just for them. Eventually as our children are
able they get the independence to take over that big dream and learn
o flourish on their own.

Moving Ahead at Our Child's Speed

I have never accepted the idea that you put your child into situations
where the odds are stacked against them and fight, but you will be
fighting the school system while they are in it. Systems as big as the
education system rarely move. If they do, it's at a snail's pace. So you
end up fighting the school most of your child's waking life, from August
through June, all the while your child is subject to the school's control.
That sounds like a recipe for disaster.

You have help to homeschool your special needs child. My husband
and I started years ago to reach out and begin building a community
of special need homeschoolers all around the world. We provide in-
dividualized help when we can. We are also reaching out to help the
community as a whole by speaking, writing, and talking with homeschooling community leaders. However I realized along the way that
those things were very good but hands on how-to type workshops,
individual sessions and now online courses needed to be developed
to help homeschoolers thrive. I am working on opening a larger online
presence because with five children that have significant health issues
I realize that babysitters and time off to attend a homeschooling conference is not a possibility for many. We were there and we hear your
need. Chris and I are moving to meet you where you are and help your
homeschooling be more successful, better suited to your child's specific learning strengths and weaknesses. Helping your home become
a more peaceful place for all.

Benefits of Homeschooling

Homeschooling has been a Godsend for my family! The flexibility of scheduling and allowing multiple doctor appointments when needed for my children. The ability to get private therapy that helped my children tremendously. Over all homeschooling is a safer option for my children and I believe yours too.

Our children are able to be home out of germ central (public school.) Most of my children are immune suppressed and they really do get every cold that they come near. We even got an odd variant of whopping cough.

Being able to stay home and learn has helped keep anxiety down and allowed my children to separate their developmental delays and other learning disability from learning solid foundational concepts.

Take for example my daughter, who has dyslexia but she is outstanding in the sciences. When she got to high school it was imperative she read the science text we had chosen for her. However the material and font were too much for her to decipher and read in a timely manner. The science curriculum we used had an audio that went with the textbook. She was then able to follow along in the book with the audio. This turned out to help her two fold. She kept up in science but she also pushed her reading abilities to a higher level.

There is another wonderful benefit of homeschooling that I didn't fully understand until years into it. The ability to share my beliefs and help guide my children towards their own relationship with the Lord. For years I was so focused on meeting their special needs that I didn't put the needed effort into their spiritual life. Thankfully Chris and I lived a very open spiritual life, prayer life, and bible study that the kids watched for years. All of our children despite the stumbling blocks of their disabilities have come to love Jesus. We now start our days with prayer and Bible study. I am thrilled to have children to share a study time with. It pulls our family together helping us strengthen our loving bonds!

Your Delightfully Different Path

The Flexibility of Homeschooling

We are blessed. The joy of homeschooling has provided a unique and very flexible lifestyle. We are able to travel often and share each and every day together. Having a disease that is life shortening and knowing the time is limited with my children, I cherish each and every day. Being able to be together through homeschooling is such a relief and a treasure.

After I had my major stroke I was extremely weak, learning to live life again with a feeding tube and my dominant right side weakened. Nurses coming and going at my house was common. We had to get inventive to keep our home going. When fall came we had to think completely out of the box for homeschooling.

I spent most of the day in my hospital bed. I was too weak to sit up at the table like we would normally do for schooling. It took some thought and modification to our home to make homeschooling work. My hospital bed was in the living room and we emptied the room of everything but an end table and my medical supplies cart. Then we placed a skinny portable table across the bottom of my bed. I was large enough the homeschooling computer could be on it. So one child could do their online work. Then there was room for two more kids to work at the table.

We made it work. The children learned and passed that year with flying colors. I have to admit there were days I wanted to just roll over and sleep after my stroke. It was a tough recovery. Having my children there waiting on me to homeschool gave me a reason to sit up and get to work. My children are a pure delight in my life. I am honored to do my best to meet their needs.

Through our times of tears and joys we have gained the ability to help other families. I don't know where our journey will take us from here but I am excited to experience the highs and be prepared with the strength of the Lord for the lows.

Homeschooling Our Unique and Wonderful Life

Along the way I realized that I wasn't just homeschooling for twelve years I was teaching my children life schooling. A way of life that is full of learning and engaging in the world in a productive almost inventive way. Homeschoolers are active, engaged, and ready to learn. I came to understand through watching my children grow and learn that I was teaching the hows and whys they should learn, question, and be curious about the world around us. I will never be able to teach my children everything but I can teach them how to learn about everything.

Many of us do not have a firm ending in sight of our homeschooling. While our public school counterparts are often cut off educationally at 18 or 21. We can continue until we feel the proper level of skills are learned or you realize that this is a long term project and your life will continue on as it has been. There is no need to fear this realization. Embrace the journey.

What is my big dream? Even with the terminal nature of my disease I dream big! I dream of helping my children fundraise to adopt their own house full of kids. I pray for years of ministry and outreach that serves the families and people we meet. We are a foodie family. We love cooking and cooking big. I have a funny cartoonish vision of a family at Thanksgiving in a big house and its full to overflowing. The table is packed and the doorbell peals. I joke that I will have to send someone out the back door to push the new comers in the front. That is my big dream to have a growing healthy family that wants to be together. I have found that as a whole my family has pulled together to become a loyal strong family that will always be there for each other. May all our homes be filled to overflowing with kindness and godly joy!

I enjoy homeschooling my children. Despite the learning disabilities and medical issues we continue to progress. Homeschooling is not a last resort option that is painful. It is a glorious step towards stronger family relationships, more focused educational material, and the extra time to grow. No matter the path set before you and your child you are on that path together as a team! I have faith in you. You Can Do It! Be persistent. Be consistent. Slow and steady does win this race and teaches us such wonderful things along the way!

Acknowledgements

A special thank you to the families that allowed me to interview them and learn how they homeschooled. And to the many readers that have been on the journey of writing this book with me since before my major stroke several years ago. Thank you for the constant encouragement and support!

God bless my friends.

The Smilie Method

Supplies:

Cardstock paper

Printer

Scissors

Laminator and laminating pouch

Velcro® dots

Directions:

Print off the Smilies and base onto cardstock.

Cut out all the pieces from the page.

Place piece in laminating pouch (as per your laminator's instructions) and laminate.

Cool. Then attach the Velcro® dots to the back of the Smilie and the base.

You can now use the base to help with teaching your child self-regulation in easy three step process, as described in chapter 6.

Additional tips: You can attach the base to the desk your child normally uses. You can even attach it to the visor in your vehicle to help with outbursts while on the road. You can change the coloring of the Smilies or the cardstock to your child's favorite color make getting a Smilie even more of a treat.

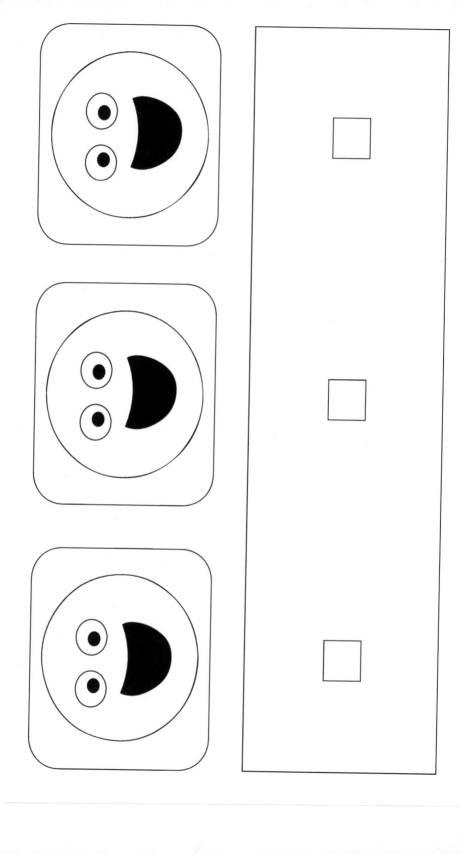

Special perks just for you!

Would you like to just download the Smilies? Other updates and related material and printables that complement *Homeschooling When Learning Isn't Easy?* Then come directly to the website: www.SpecialNeedsHomeschooling.com/bookperks or email us at admin@specialneedshomeschooling.com

Special Needs Homeschooling—Heather and Christopher Laurie Are Ready to Speak Near You!

Would you like the Special Needs Homeschooling team of Heather and/or Christopher?

Speaking at conventions, support groups, church retreats to help your family excel!

Topics from special needs, homeschooling, marriage in difficult time, to end of life discussions from a Christian perspective and more.

For details about speaking opportunities and topics please go to www.specialneedshomeschooling.com/speaking.

You can join the community:

Website members' area
Facebook: /specialneedshomeschooling
Twitter: /SpecialNeedsHS

You can find us on other social media platforms like Pinterest, Youtube, Periscope, and Instagram.

Contact Us:

726 East Park Ave Pmb 280
Fairmont, West Virginia 26554
admin@specialneedshomeschoooling.com
www.specialneedshomeschooling.com

Made in the USA
San Bernardino, CA
13 November 2017